ACKNOWLEDGMENTS

Special thanks to the authors, editors, art directors, copy editors, and other staff members of *Fine Homebuilding* and *Inspired House* who contributed to the development of the articles in this book.

Contents

How Much Space Do You Really Need?

BY SARAH SUSANKA

After having written the series of Not-So-Big-House books, I get a lot of questions from people who want to know how much house is enough. They want rules and standards to answer the question.

I respond to these inquiries with two general statements. First, making a house with a sense of home has almost nothing to do with square footage. And second, my ideas behind a Not-So-Big house usually mean building a house about a third smaller than you thought you needed but one that is just as expensive. Both of these comments are intended to take the focus off quantity and place it firmly on the things that affect livability—the quality and character of the spaces we inhabit.

In your remodel

That all sounds well and good, but how do you implement those noble goals when you're remodeling? Where do you start, and how do you know whether the amount of space you are living in or plan to live in is too big or too small or just right? The guidelines in the sidebar at right are intended to help determine whether it's more quantity of space you need or more quality you're really seeking.

Our typical solution these days is to favor quantity over quality, when almost without exception it's an

> ### WHAT TO CONSIDER WHEN YOU'RE REMODELING
>
> - Identify the problem areas and rooms.
> - Take an inventory of the rooms you already have, including dimensions and frequency of use.
> - Look for spaces that can be connected to meet your needs.
> - Look for spaces that can do double duty.
> - Only after these steps, consider adding on.
> - The scale of any added space should match that of the existing house.

increase in quality of living environment that really makes us feel better, more comfortable, and more at home.

To orient and ground our discussion, let's look at a family with plans to remodel. An advantage they had—particularly over a family considering building an all-new house—is that they lived daily with their home's shortcomings, so they were painfully aware of where its shape and size collided with the household's needs.

Although they may not have been able to devise the perfect solution, they could see the problems they were facing with great clarity. Their challenge was to avoid jumping to the simplest and most obvious solution, which very likely would have been too big and might even have spoiled the character and utility of the existing space.

On pp. 4–5 you'll see the before and after floor plans of the remodel of the Baer family's house.

In your new house

If you are considering building a new house you might imagine that the issues are similar; however, the challenges related to figuring out how much space you will need in a new home are significantly greater than determining space needs when you are remodeling.

The reason for this is that the homeowners of the house to be remodeled can tell you right away what works and what doesn't in their existing home, which opens a seemingly easy discussion of how to make it better with renovation.

For a couple thinking about a new home, the plans for their potential building project that they look at on paper typically don't give them enough information to gauge what the space will feel like when construction is complete. Reading a set of plans is one thing—it's fairly easy to understand architects' drawing conventions once they're explained to you—but lots of people have a hard time visualizing, for example, how big a 14-ft. by 16-ft. room will feel. New-home builders can't kick the tires until the house is well on its way to completion, so there's a lot of guesswork involved.

Because there's an almost universal fear of feeling cramped—what I have termed "fear of too smallness"—would-be homeowners will tend to make everything a bit bigger than their favored plan suggests, just to be on the safe side. This is one of the primary reasons our culture's new houses keep escalating in size. It's based on a fear of having the opposite problem, with the result that many households find themselves at sea in an ocean of space that is never too small but also never too comfortable.

On pp. 6–7 we'll look at the floor plan for the Winston household's existing house and the floor plan for the new house they want to build.

WHAT TO CONSIDER WHEN YOU'RE BUILDING NEW

- Measure and inventory the rooms you live in now and identify dimensions and frequency of use.
- As you look at plans to build, or as you work with an architect, keep the proportions of your existing home in mind.
- Don't build spaces you use less than a handful of times a year.
- Identify rooms that can do double duty.
- Select a design whose proportions match those of your favorite houses.
- Always get measurements of the spaces you plan to build, including the ceiling height of each, before committing to a design.
- If you think something might be too big, try to find a model home with similar proportions to visit to see how it makes you feel.
- Find someone you can trust to help you with the design and then listen to what he or she advises.

ADDING SPACE BUT NOT MUCH SQUARE FOOTAGE

JOHN AND CINDY BAER live in a fine old Victorian with their three young children. The house is beautiful, but the space on the main floor was poorly suited to their needs. They spent most of their time while at home either cooped up in the inhospitable kitchen or sitting around the formal dining room table inherited from Cindy's mom, worrying all the while about whether the children would damage it.

They wanted a new kitchen, an informal eating area, a place for the kids to play or watch TV while Cindy was in the kitchen, and an in-home office on the main level. The remodeled floor plan involves very little additional square footage, but it does give the family lots more room.

THE PROBLEMS

1 An awkward rear entry delivers people directly into the kitchen.

2 The half-bath has only a toilet and a sink, so there's no reason for it to be as large as it is.

3 The circa 1975 kitchen is where most of the family living occurs.

4 The dining room is isolated, making it difficult to use. The heirloom table isn't appropriate for family use.

5 The large entry hall is wasted space because the family always uses the back door.

6 The living room is rarely used because it is too formal for everyday purposes.

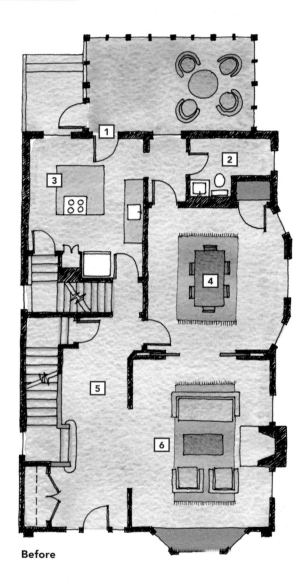

Before

THE SOLUTIONS

1. A new informal eating area with a great view of the backyard was added to the kitchen.

2. Bigger kitchen windows provide a better connection to the backyard.

3. The size of the screened porch was reduced and a new back entry created.

4. The half-bath was reduced in size to make room for a mudroom.

5. A 2-ft. bumpout provides room for a counter without having to move the basement stairs, which would have been expensive. There is no window on this side because of the proximity of the neighbors.

6. A section of the wall was removed to create a connection between the kitchen and the dining room.

7. A computer desk was added to the dining room, making it a multipurpose room. Bookshelves are on the opposite wall.

8. The heirloom table has a new protective covering, so it can be used for homework and bill paying, as well as for dining.

9. A small table and chairs in the living room provides a spot for card games and jigsaw puzzles.

10. Bookshelves on four walls make the room feel more comfortable and less formal.

11. A flat-screen TV above the fireplace is a new attraction to the living room.

12. The furniture is rearranged to make it more user friendly.

13. An upholstered cushion on the window seat creates a comfortable, cozy nook.

14. Because mail is delivered at the front of the house, this is a perfect place for a mail-sorting center.

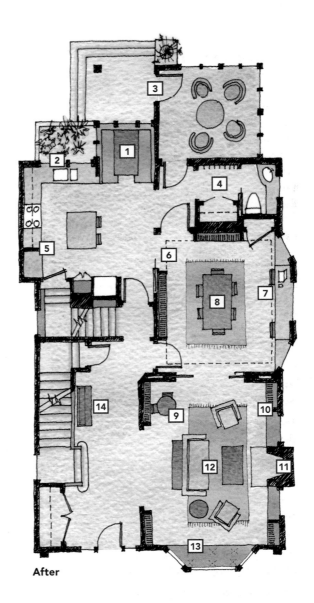

After

THE WINSTON FAMILY'S SPACE

DOUG AND JULIE WINSTON and their 13-year-old daughter Laura have lived in a rather drab 1950s two-story house for 12 years. Although there's easily enough space in it for three, the kitchen has always been a problem, with very little counter space and no place to eat without retiring to the dining room. They like to entertain, so a dining room that can be used to serve two to four guests is important. Their current dining room is OK, but a little on the small size and without much to recommend it aesthetically. The living room is large but not used much because it's not in the primary circulation path through the house. Instead, the den, which opens off the dining room, is their primary living space. They like it because its size is comfortable for the three of them to gather and socialize. They'd like a new house with more character, one that makes family interaction easier during food prep but that still allows them to engage in different activities, such as homework, reading, and listening to music, within a shared living space.

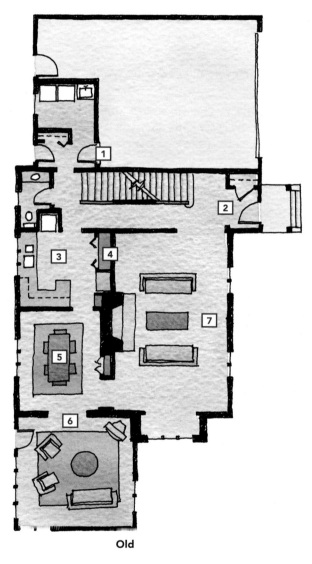

Old

THE OLD HOUSE

1 The back of the house is the main entry point for family members, and it's ugly, cramped, and unwelcoming.

2 The front entry is dark and cramped.

3 The kitchen is small and awkward, with limited counter space and no informal eating area.

4 The pantry is one feature that works.

5 The formal dining room is completely separate from the kitchen. Most meals are eaten in the den.

6 The den, where most of the living in the house happens, is too far from the kitchen for easy communication during food prep.

7 The formal living room is rarely used. It's by far the biggest room, but it's not easily visible from the lived-in areas of the house.

THE NEW HOUSE

1 The one living area is comfortable and appropriate for both everyday living and formal occasions.

2 A flat-screen TV is mounted above the fireplace.

3 The office/away room can be separated acoustically by closing the door, but it remains connected visually to the living area with an interior window.

4 The formal dining room does double duty as library and homework area.

5 A library alcove offers a quiet, cozy place to read.

6 The kitchen has plenty of counter space, a walk-in pantry, and connection to surrounding spaces.

7 The breakfast bar offers a place to socialize during meal preparation.

8 The informal eating area has a lovely view and a strong connection to the kitchen.

9 The small back deck connects with the garden.

10 The pleasant and light-filled front entry has an overlook from the kitchen half a level above.

11 The family entry also opens to the welcoming front foyer.

12 Dotted lines indicate ceiling-height change.

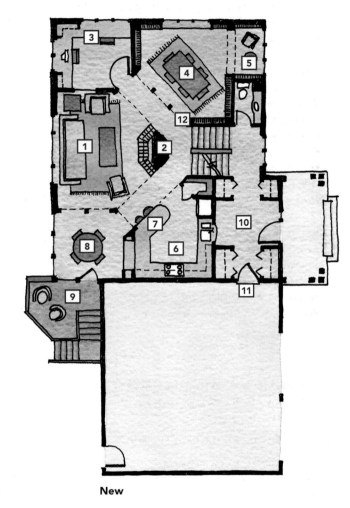

New

Cabins

A Big Little House on the Ridge

BY JONATHAN WHITE

GLIMPSED FROM THE PATH, the Kimball house is the epitome of a shelter in the woods: a gable roof and a chimney. Photo taken at A on floor plan.

Jay and Sue Kimball had dreams of building a pair of houses on a ridge overlooking the sheltered bay that occupies the heart of Washington's Orcas Island. One house would be the primary residence, and the other a Craftsman-style cabin for visitors. With architect in hand, they set about designing the guest cabin first. But midway into the building process an unexpected change in Jay and Sue's work life turned everything on end. As a result, they moved to the island sooner than they had anticipated, putting plans for the main house on hold and making the cabin their primary residence.

As it turned out, the cabin became a lesson in efficiency. It has no wasted space, offering lessons on how any small house can make the most of the space under, and in this case, next to its roof.

The roof is more than just a lid

To get the project off to the right start, architect Roy Lundgren asked Jay and Sue to write a narrative describing their vision of the guest cabin. In their detailed and lively articulation, Sue described open, light-filled spaces clad in wood and serving multiple functions. She wanted room to dance and nooks to nestle into with a good book. Jay felt strongly about building the house with as little disturbance to the land as possible.

The first impression of the Kimball house is all roof. Visitors park about 50 steps away and descend on a winding footpath through mature trees and mossy nurse logs. The roof's long overhangs, thick-butt cedar shingles, and stone chimney emulate the textures of the forested hillside. The true complexity of the roof, however, is revealed only moments before you knock on the front door. "Let the bones show," asked Jay, and indeed they do.

Gazing upward, the eye is captured by a fabric of timber that forms the roof's underbelly. Soaring overhangs—8 ft. at the eaves and nearly 12 ft. at the gable—are supported by hefty cantilevered rafters. On top of these structures rests a lacework of purlins and cedar planking, each layer woven perpendicular to the last, and each descending in size. Inspired by Japanese architecture, the result is a cabin with a visual field of ever-changing light and depth.

"Long roof overhangs create a strong sense of shelter," Lundgren says, "which is really what a house is all about. They invite you in and enhance the feeling of protection." In mild and rainy climates such as that of Orcas Island, large overhangs also extend the living space and protect the house from weather.

Below the front gable a triangular deck pokes out and over a precipitous west-facing slope. Thoughtful pruning gives the feeling of privacy and safety while creating corridors of dazzling views.

The secrets to a function-packed floor plan

The heart of Sue and Jay's house is a 24-sq.-ft. space with a cathedral ceiling that rises to 16 ft. in the center (see the photo on p. 12). Within this symmetrical room are a number of discrete areas for a home office, a living area, a dining space, a kitchen, a master bedroom, and a carpeted inglenook in front of the fire (see the floor plan at right).

The main floor includes the kitchen, dining area, and living room. Exposed rafters topped with tongue-and-groove pine planking mirror the rustic details of the exterior. The conventional ridge beam is absent, leaving the interior peak sharp and unclut-

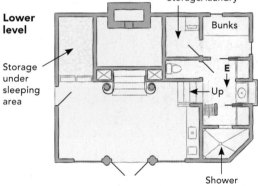

Specs

Bedrooms: None really, but sleeps 6
Bathrooms: 1
Size: 800 sq. ft.
Cost: $431 per sq. ft.
Completed: 2002
Location: Eagle Ridge, Orcas Island, Washington
Architects: Street, Lundgren & Foster
Builder: White Construction Co.; David Klein, foreman

Photos taken at lettered positions.

0 2 4   8 ft.

NO WASTED SPACE

In this floor plan, discrete spaces for specific functions abound. Their boundaries are level changes, circulation paths, and even the placement of the beams that carry the rafters near the ridge. Because the spaces are open to one another, there is no sense of confinement in this house. Built-in cabinets divide the living area and kitchen from the sleeping area and office, doing double duty as half-walls and storage.

A ROOF THAT SHELTERS INSIDE AND OUT. A 12-ft.-deep overhang at the entry is composed of layers of rafters and purlins inspired by Japanese architecture. The roof overhang makes the deck an all-year outdoor room. Photo taken at C on floor plan.

tered and allowing the massive fireplace chimney to rise directly through the center of the building.

The gable at the entry is tall and made mostly of glass, enabling the expansive views and un-obstructed sunlight to chase away a sense of separation between inside and out. Double doors in the center of this wall beckon toward the deck.

Five steps lead from the main floor to the loft. The stairs are flanked at their base by a pair of Douglas-fir columns, salvaged from the bottom of the Columbia River. These rough, deeply checked logs stand out in contrast to the adjacent refined surfaces of vertical-grain fir and glass. A steel handrail, fashioned by Steve Gropp of Salamander Forge, spirals up these columns like the tendrils of a climbing vine.

At the top of the stairs stands the centerpiece of the house: a massive Rumford fireplace. By day a ridge skylight spills natural light down its rusticated

A HANDRAIL FORGED IN FIRE.
Sinewy, vinelike tendrils of hand-tooled steel wrap around the railing to the upper level.

COMPLEX ON THE INSIDE.
Centered on the ridge, a skylight pours raking light across the stone chimney and hearth. Note how the rafters cantilever over the beams adjacent to the chimney, eliminating the need for a light-blocking ridge beam. Photo taken at B on floor plan.

face of edge-cliff stone; by night, dimmable pendants provide a sharper focus of light and shadow. "Because we have a lot of overcast days in the Northwest," Lundgren says, "our local light tends to be soft and gray. I find that natural light from a skylight, far more than a window, reveals the true form of the interior space."

Built-in seats on each side of the fireplace are carpeted with black wool and serve at times for reading or eating by a warm fire and at other times as steps to the adjacent platforms. The one to the right of the fireplace is used as an office and the other is just big enough for Jay and Sue's sleeping futon. Below the futon platform is a storage room, which is accessed by a secret door in the living-room bookshelf.

The kitchen takes up a scant 8 ft. of wall space, but within these confines Sue got what she needed. The cabinets are grain-matched clear fir, the floors are Spanish cherry, and the countertops are black Corian® with an undermount stainless-steel sink. A mirror backsplash gives the illusion of windows that are located under the upper cabinets.

To maximize counter space, Jay and Sue installed Sub-Zero® refrigerator drawers and a two-burner

cooktop. Without the flexibility of a typical four-burner stove, they have adapted to a more efficient approach to cooking, which works fine for the two of them. For dinner parties, though, they expand operations to the gas grill and the big worktable on the deck under the eaves. For baking they rely on the multitasking GE Advantium® wall-mounted oven (see the sidebar at left).

COOKING WITH THE GE ADVANTIUM 120

OUR KITCHEN HAS LIMITED SPACE, so we installed an electric oven: the GE Advantium 120. At 15½ in. deep by 30 in. wide by 16½ in. high, it fits comfortably into the upper cabinets. The Advantium plugs into a standard 120v outlet and includes an exhaust vent that clears the air for both the cooktop and the oven. But we didn't appreciate the Advantium's most important attributes until we actually used it.

The Advantium has three cooking modes: convection, microwave, and Speedcook. In Speedcook mode, the oven heats with the speed of a microwave and broils and browns like a conventional oven.

The Advantium uses interchangeable turntables—one glass, one metal—depending on cooking mode. To use our 13½-in. by 21-in. casserole, we remove the turntable, set the oven on convection mode, and simply rotate the casserole halfway through cooking. We've used the Speedcook feature and can verify that it will bake a potato with crispy skin in 12 minutes. But truth be known, we mostly use the oven in the convection mode. It is a compact workhorse. We routinely prepare meals for six or more people.

—Sue and Jay Kimball

UPPER-LEVEL BEDROOM AND OFFICE. Carpeted benches on each side of the inglenook lead to the bed alcove on one side and to the office on the other. Built-in cabinets throughout the house maximize storage while minimizing the need for space-consuming furniture. A small sofa, two end tables, and a narrow dining table are the only freestanding furniture in the building. Photo taken at D on floor plan.

A MOSTLY INDOOR KITCHEN. At 8 ft. long, the kitchen packs a lot of function into a small space. Two under-counter refrigerator drawers are on the left side. A two-burner cooktop and an Advantium oven in the upper cabinets anchor the right side. When more firepower is required, the gas grill on the deck is pressed into service. Photo taken at F on floor plan.

A BATHROOM OF MANY PARTS. Reached by way of a ladder, a sunny loft over the shower is illuminated by its own skylight. Photo taken at E on floor plan.

Bunk beds and the bath round out the lower level

Stairs that are off the kitchen lead five steps down to the tiled floor of the bathroom, which is adjacent to and below the spaces for guests.

A loft above the shower is a favorite sleeping nook for visiting nieces and nephews. On the lower level, a second pair of bunk beds accommodates more guests. Behind the bunk room, the walk-in closet includes a stacked washer and dryer.

After two years in the house, Jay and Sue have few complaints. "I miss a bathtub," says Sue, "and privacy with overnight guests can be a challenge. But I've come to value the small size, aesthetically, practically, and environmentally. The house brings together a sense of calm—like what I feel in a small chapel—and a tree-house-like playfulness that comes from our location in the woods. There's a wonderful sense of discovery here."

Raising the Baby Barn

BY PETER KURT WOERNER

In the late 1980s I bought 10 acres of hillside in southern Vermont and moved a big antique barn onto the property for a vacation house. I left most of the site wooded but cleared 3 acres, creating a meadow with nice views to the east.

By 1995 I got the urge to build again. This time I wanted to build a small guesthouse that would echo the main house. I had the perfect place for what I call the "Baby Barn," nestled against the tree line overlooking the meadow and far enough from the big barn for privacy.

To control costs, I wanted the Baby Barn to be relatively simple. I planned to put the finishing touches on it working mostly solo on weekends, with occasional extended sessions. If the house was too complex, I'd never get it done. On the other hand, I wanted to create a variety of spaces, both intimate and expansive, and to use reclaimed barn timbers and siding to emulate the warmth and richness of an old structure (www.conklinsbarnwood.com).

The sloped-site advantage

The Baby Barn is based on a traditional New England bank barn, which is built into a slope and typically has two floors. The upper floor opens to the uphill side and vice versa. Placing the Baby Barn on a slope allowed me to save some money on a foundation and to have daylight in the downhill lower-level rooms.

The main floor has one big space for living and dining, a kitchen, a bedroom, a loft over the bedroom, and a bathroom (see the floor plan on p. 18). There is no formal entry with a closet, just pegs for coats.

The primary rectangle of the foundation is 18 ft. by 40 ft. I chose 18 ft. so that I could use 2×12 floor joists and not pay extra for I-joists (I don't mind the floor being a little bouncy). The living room feels quite generous because of the 12-ft. walls and 10-ft.-high windows.

On the lower level, the mechanicals and the laundry are on the windowless uphill side of the barn. Next to this area is a central stair and hallway with a shared bath for the two bedrooms that open to the meadow by way of French doors.

Hard work, smart choices accelerate move-in day

My goal was to start in May and have the house weathertight, insulated, heated, and livable (vacation style) with one working bathroom by Thanksgiving. I hired a full-time carpenter and two helpers for

SIMPLE BUILDING, GREAT VARIETY. From the intimate dining deck off the kitchen to the 20-ft.-high living room, the Baby Barn packs a lot of different spaces into a small house. Photo taken at B on floor plan.

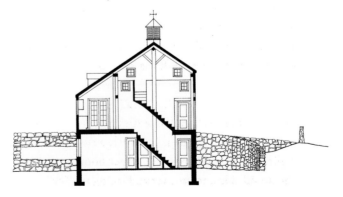

this big-push stage of the project, and I did all of the ordering of materials and coordinating of subs even though I live three hours away.

I spent money strategically, investing in high-quality finish items but also saving on components that would be easy to change later. For example, the windows are from Pella's® Architect Series, and the roof is covered with western red-cedar shingles. On the other hand, the first kitchen I put into the Baby Barn was made of CDX plywood cabinets that I built in a day and a cast-iron sink that I found in a dumpster. This camp kitchen worked fine for the

THE BANK BARN REBORN

Notched into a hillside and having entries on two levels, the Baby Barn is a direct descendant of the venerable bank barn.

Ground floor

← North

Bedroom

Mechanicals

Master bedroom

Laundry

B

Main floor

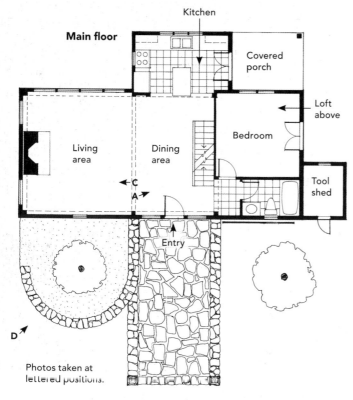

Kitchen

Covered porch

Loft above

Living area

Dining area

Bedroom

Tool shed

C

A

Entry

D

Photos taken at lettered positions.

0   5   10   20 ft.

Specs

Bedrooms: 3, plus sleeping loft
Bathrooms: 2
Size: 1,700 sq. ft.
Cost: $100 per sq. ft.
Completed: 2000
Location: South Londonderry, Vermont
Designer/builder: Peter Kurt Woerner, FAIA

A RAMP COMPOSED OF FIELDSTONE LEADS TO THE MAIN ENTRYWAY. A barn door with a cutout for the bathroom window seals off the French doors between visits. Photo taken at D on floor plan.

first three years, until I had the time and resources to put in a proper one.

To simplify the mechanical systems I chose a direct-vent, propane-fired hot-air furnace and hot-water supply. This saved me the time and money required to build a masonry flue for a conventional oil-fired boiler.

I would choose direct-vent gas appliances again, but I would approach the electric service differently. Because I went with gas for heating, I decided I could save a little money by installing a 100-amp service panel. It has worked fine so far, though if I decide to add a garage I'll likely have to upgrade the electric service. In retrospect, I should have spent the extra money for a 200-amp panel.

The plan worked. By Thanksgiving I had the Baby Barn weathertight, plumbed, and rough-wired. With a three-burner camp stove, a tub with a poly shower curtain, and some tag-sale furniture, voilà, the house was livable.

Fireplaces as centerpieces

I love fireplaces, so I put one in the master bedroom and another directly above it in the living room. The raised stone hearth in the living room accommodates firewood storage underneath. By stacking the fireplaces, I needed only one chimney. I kept all the firebox and chimney masonry inside the building envelope for two reasons: one, so that I could work on them in any type of weather; and two, to save energy. Why build a fireplace outside the building envelope when all the masonry will be exposed to low temperatures (especially in Vermont, where it can be as cold as 45°F below zero)?

I built the fireplaces myself out of concrete block. Both are Count Rumford designs, which are great for looks and for throwing off heat. I did, however, have a mason take the chimney through the roof for me. Then I spent a couple of years covering the block with stone veneer.

Long-term projects have their advantages

As you get to know a house over time, opportunities present themselves that aren't always obvious in the big push to finalize a plan. As the Baby Barn grew up, I got to customize it—in 1950s hot-rod parlance—with some bolt-on goodies. Three in particular stand out.

BARN DOOR

During framing I thought it would be neat to have a sliding barn door to cover up the three French entry doors, both for security and, for lack of a better word, "barnishness." So I built a 10-ft. by 10-ft. barn door in the living room. It wasn't until I had finished the door that I realized it wouldn't fit diagonally through the French-door opening. A classic screw-up. I got off light, though, because I hadn't put up the siding yet. I cut a slot in the plywood sheathing and slid the door through it.

CUPOLA

The building was looking a little too plain, even for a minimalist like me. A cupola is a classic detail on a bank barn, where it serves as a vent. I thought it would be pretty cool to have one over the dining room for day lighting; at night, it would shine like a beacon.

To avoid a repeat of the barn-door fiasco, I carefully designed a cupola that could fit through the double doors in the kitchen. I built the cupola in the living room, minus its base, and finished it inside and out with cedar shingles. I then got up on the roof and used a chainsaw to chop a hole so that I could build the cupola's base in place.

On a nice late-spring day we had a cupola-raising party. The local lumber company donated its crane truck, we lifted up the cupola, and it dropped in place perfectly.

UNDER A RUSTIC SKIN, HIGH-PERFORMANCE INSULATION. Recycled barn-board paneling and hand-hewn timbers set the tone. Polyisocyanurate foam insulation behind the paneling keeps the rooms comfy. At the top of the stairs, a sleeping loft overlooks the living room. Photo taken at A on floor plan.

A LOFTY SPACE WITH DISTANT VIEWS. Banks of windows reach to nearly 12 ft. above the living-room floor. Wide spruce planks carry on the rustic feel of the recycled barn-board paneling. Photo taken at C on floor plan.

COVERED PORCH

Originally there was an 8-ft. by 12-ft. notch in the southeast corner of the house, next to the kitchen. A year or two after the Baby Barn was up I started thinking about how nice it would be to have a covered porch for dining alfresco. With just a corner post, a bit of roof, and some decking there would be room for a little table.

Working with a top-notch framer, we completed the porch in three days and feathered some new cedar shingles into the old roof. I also added a quirky little dormer, which brings light to both the porch and the sleeping loft.

Obviously, building a house this way is not for everyone. A vacation house can be doable, and if you're young you might be able to take a similar approach to building a permanent residence. Stress on a relationship can be severe, though, so it's critical to have a few construction-free zones, especially a clean bathroom and a tidy place to sleep. The sweat-equity savings are significant, but the key to it all is to remember that life is in the living.

Did Starting Small Work Out?

BY ROBERT KNIGHT

In the late 1990s my firm designed two projects that tackled the problem of how to start using your land when you're not ready to spend the money for your dream house. This story is about how one of them, a little Greek-revival farmhouse that was phase 1 of a larger home, worked out.

When they bought their land, Chris and Bette Noble were committed to living part of the year in Maine, with an eye toward eventually living there full-time.

Initially we designed a Greek-revival farmhouse that pleased all of us (see the drawing at right). By our calculations, however, it was going to cost around $350,000. Although that figure would be affordable for the Nobles at some point, it wasn't in the cards in the late 1990s, so we decided to build the house in two phases. Phase 1 (see the photo at right and drawing on p. 25) consisted of a main room with a kitchen and space for sitting and a dining table. A ladder in this room led to a loft over the screened porch.

The bedroom/bath, known as the "dependency," sat on piers and was bolted to the south end of the

STARTING POINT, WEST ELEVATION

The original plan was to build the Greek-revival farmhouse shown above, but to do it in two stages beginning with the one-story portion.

PHASE 1 (1998) Bedrooms: 1; Bathrooms: 1; Size: 714 sq. ft.; Cost: $112 per sq. ft.

PHASE 2 (2006) Bedrooms: 2; Bathrooms: 2; Size: 1,248 sq. ft.; Cost: $232 per sq. ft.

PHASE 3 (2010) Home office; Size: 216 sq. ft.; Cost: $273 per sq. ft.; Total: 2,178 sq. ft.

PHASE 2

PHASE 1

COMFY CAMP FOR EIGHT YEARS. The main room had a temporary kitchen and dining corner during phase 1 (above). People were so fond of this space and its unfinished quality that there was resistance to finishing the house. Photos taken at A on floor plan.

main room. The plan was to unbolt the dependency during phase 2, move it into the woods, and expand it to become a guest cottage. Then we would convert the main room into a dedicated living room with a fireplace and fill in the rest of the three-bedroom house as planned.

It didn't work out that way.

Instead, the house went through the same kind of evolution that Maine farmhouses in the 19th century underwent. The family's needs changed, and indeed even the family changed (see the sidebar on pp. 24–25).

Eight years on

The idea of getting on the land really worked. For eight years the house was used on weekends and for longer summer stays. When it came time to go to phase 2, though, the new Nobles decided they didn't need three bedrooms and didn't want a guesthouse. We moved the dependency around to the east and added enough space to it to make a downstairs bedroom and office accessible by wheelchair (see the floor plans on p. 25). The house got shorter and turned a corner, and the living room was dressed up and fitted with a fireplace.

CHANGES HAPPEN

IN THE EARLY 1990S I visited the Nobles on their newly purchased land and photographed their tent. Bette Noble, Chris's wife and my friend, died in 2002, and a year later I returned to visit the warm, rustic phase 1 house.

Love brought the major changes to our lives and the house. In 2004 Chris and I began redesigning phase 2 with Knight Associates, my introduction to working with architects and contractors. I had no idea there was so much to say about so many details! Turning the corner with the new ell would provide a private first-floor bedroom and bathroom, an intimate outdoor space, and new views of the Bagaduce River. I had bonded with the dependency, so instead of setting it aside as a future guest house, we decided to incorporate it into the house as my home office.

Bob Knight had warned us about expecting a guest room to serve as a home office, and it wasn't long before I began to dream of having an area where I could continue working even when guests arrived. We sat down with the architects and designed a bright studio/project room with a high ceiling that links us to the woods and the nearby stream. One exterior door opens to the back porch, and an interior door goes into the guest room, eliminating the need for an additional bathroom. When guests are here we leave the studio via the back-porch door and enter the door to the main house, preserving our guests' privacy. The resulting addition looks as if it has always been here.

—Christine Farrow-Noble, freelance writer and photographer

THE STARTING POINT
Conceived as a three-bedroom house, the initial plan was prioritized into two phases to make the project more affordable.

Ground floor

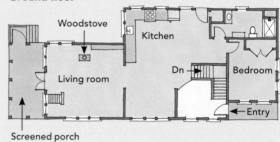

◄North

0 2 4 8 ft.

Second floor

PHASE 1

Phase 1 consisted of the living room/screened porch portion of the house, plus the "dependency": a removable bedroom on piers.

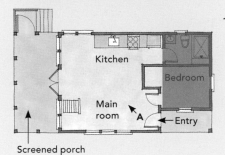

Kitchen

Bedroom

Main room

A

Entry

Screened porch

PHASE 2

Phase 2 deviated from the original plan. The dependency turned the corner, becoming a home office/guest bedroom.

Ground floor

Deck

Bedroom

Kitchen

Living room

Dining area

A

Up

Covered porch

Entry

Screened porch

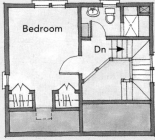

Bedroom

Dn

Second floor

PHASE 3

Phase 3 added a dedicated office/studio, a concession to the fact that an office/guest bedroom just doesn't work once guests arrive. Larry Packwood Builders constructed all three phases.

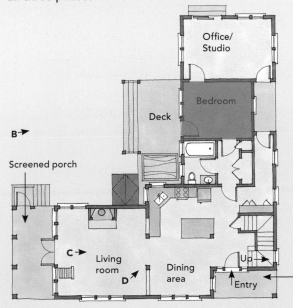

Office/ Studio

Bedroom

Deck

B

Screened porch

C

Living room

D

Dining area

Up

Entry

Covered porch

1998   2006   2010

PHASE 3 COMPLETE. The new room at the far left of the house, a dedicated office and project studio, supplied the missing piece of the puzzle. The gable roof makes a proper conclusion to this one-story wing. Photo taken at B on floor plan.

The drawing above left shows the original version looking back from the water; the middle drawing shows what we ended up with at the end of phase 2 in 2006. Would I have done it exactly this way if we had built it all at once? Probably not, because this design is a bit more complex than it needs to be to accomplish the program. However, it created better exterior spaces and gave the house a stronger elevation from up the hill on the approach. It has more of that feel of an evolved farmhouse—and that's because it did evolve—and I don't think it looks like a house and an addition.

But wait—there's more

As the house became more "home" for the Nobles and as their place in the city started to recede into the status of the "other place" they discovered that they needed to have more space. Not bedrooms— they were right about that—but they had underestimated the space and privacy they would need for work when they were here more of the time.

For some reason many clients seem loath to admit their need for a real home office, and they say to me, "My office can double as the second guest bedroom." Really? Having houseguests is not made more pleasant by having your ability to do your work canceled by their presence. Because the Nobles needed a dedicated workspace for writing and other projects, we added another piece on the "ell" (see the floor plans on p. 25). The trick was to use this extension to give the ell an endpoint—and that mostly would be accomplished by how the roof was treated.

After first trying a simple extension of the hip (boring) and then removing the hip and putting a gable on the end (looked like a double-wide had run into the building), I realized that this new piece, rather than being hidden, needed to make its own statement. So we turned its roof perpendicular to the existing ridge of the ell and created a miniature Greek temple to end the building (see the photo above and drawing above right).

Of course, we'll be in trouble if we need to extend this house again, but I probably can let my successor worry about that.

IT LOOKS LIKE IT'S ALWAYS BEEN THIS WAY. Phase 1 and phase 2 come together at the columned wall between the living room and the kitchen/dining area (below). For the first eight years the kitchen occupied the space now given over to the fireplace and its hearth (left). Photos taken at C and D on floor plan.

Watch Island Retreat

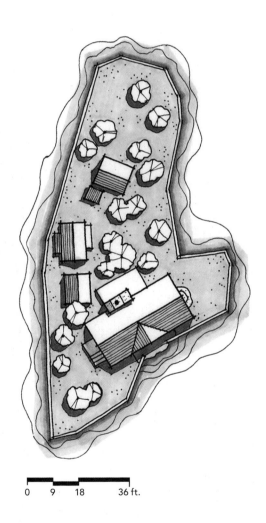

If the best getaways are the least accessible, then Bruce Danning's Watch Island in New York's Oseetah Lake certainly qualifies. It's a 10-minute boat ride in the summer, unless the water is too low. And in winter, when the ice is thick, Danning has to ski, snowmobile, or when all else fails, walk across the lake.

But Danning never thinks twice about making the trip. He purchased the island in 1985, unaware that it was too small to qualify as "buildable property." After waiting two years for the necessary permits, Danning spent the next five building the camp.

With its twig-work trim and rough-hewn siding, the main cabin looks like a simple, rustic dwelling. The inside, though, feels more like a tiny yacht club. Seven-ft.-tall mahogany windows line the walls, and the ceiling is coffered with mirrored panels. The hand-cut sandstone of the cabin's fireplace was dragged by sled over the frozen wintertime lake to the island. Danning brought over the seven species of wood used in the cabin's construction, materials he had saved from his millwork shop.

Solar panels and a wind generator answer the island's electricity needs, but Danning still hasn't found a solution to the high water that sometimes

0   9   18   36 ft.

covers the lawn, or to the muskrats and beavers that undermine the buildings and create cave-ins. Still, neither rodents nor floods keep Danning from making the trek to his remote island retreat.

BRUCE DANNING WANTED LIVING ON THE TINY ISLAND to feel like "staying on a yacht." He also was inspired by the great camps of the Adirondacks. The result is a rustic exterior with twig-work gables and trim and an ornate interior with fine wood details, including nine 3-ft. by 7-ft. mahogany windows originally intended for a Manhattan brownstone.

ON AN ISLAND ONLY AS BIG AS A LARGE HOUSE (4,400 SQ. FT.), Bruce Danning has managed to fit five buildings: the main cabin, a bunkhouse that sleeps four, his sleeping cabin, a "comfort station" with a shower, and a privy.

Nestled in the Trees

It was around the time of the Civil War that Geoffrey Prentiss's great-grandfather homesteaded several hundred acres on Washington State's San Juan Island. One hundred twenty years later, Prentiss, an architect, designed a post-and-beam, cedar-sided cabin on the land for himself and his two brothers. A long porch flanks two sides of the house and looks down to the Pacific Ocean several hundred yards away—close enough to see the waves and hear seals barking and playing on the rocky shore. Seattle-based Prentiss stays at the cabin about eight nights every month. "I have an old oak table that used to be my grandmother's," he says. "I move it out to the porch and sit with my back to the fire and work on my computer."

Perched on a hill overlooking the Pacific, the cabin is filled with windows—360 square panes of glass in total—and pairs of French doors that fill the rooms with soft light from the surrounding forest. A large open first-floor room terminates at one end in the kitchen and at the other with a fireplace (which is backed by an outdoor hearth on the adjacent porch). Sleeping lofts and balconies at each end of the building are reached by steep stairs.

A woodstove provides most of the heat, but there are back-up electric baseboards to take off the chill until the stove starts cooking. "By the end of the first day," says Prentiss, "the radiant heat from the fireplace and the woodstove are enough to keep me warm."

Below the main room, the lower level was originally designed as a large bunkroom and small bath for kids, but, Prentiss says, "It's just now being redone to have a nicer bath, a studio area, and a bedroom."

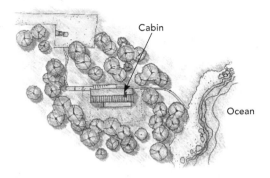

Cabin

Ocean

GEOFFREY PRENTISS'S 16-FT. BY 60-FT. CEDAR-SIDED CABIN, nestled in the trees a few hundred yards from the shore, is sited so that it can take advantage of the sun's rays. Inside (right) is one large room with sleeping lofts at both ends.

THE CONCRETE FIREPLACE IS THE HEART OF THE CABIN. After it cured, it was sanded to a satin-smooth finish. The fireplace and a woodstove provide most of the cabin's heat.

A Place to Read and Relax

BY ANNE COREY

Architect Mark Simon is also a sculptor and a woodworker. His commission to design a small retreat set in a grassy marshland gave him the opportunity to work with craftsmen skilled in the traditions of Adirondack furniture making and log-cabin building.

Though it evokes the romantic Adirondack style, this playful cabin was conceived with art in mind. Sculptural qualities are evident in the asymmetrical arrangement of logs that frame the front and back porches, as well as in the copper and tree-trunk fireplace, which creates a favored place to sit with a good book. Wide tree-trunk steps welcome visitors to the cabin, and inside, the room is filled with light from a wall of glass that makes this tiny house feel larger. Log beams above the main room give the interior perimeter an octagonal shape. "The octagon centers you," says Simon. Along with the wall of French doors, "It gives you the feeling of being at the edge of the wild, looking out in every direction."

To avoid damage to the ecologically sensitive marsh, much of the tiny cabin was built off-site. After driving piles into the marsh, carpenters secured a platform to the wood posts 4 ft. above the ground. The cabin was then brought to the site and assembled like Lincoln Logs®. Finishing touches—such as the copper-clad fireplace and three sets of French doors—were added at the site.

THE CABIN'S NOTCHED-LOG WALLS WILL SHRINK as they continue to dry, a process that will take about ten years. Bolts at the top and bottom of the cabin must be tightened every year as the logs cure.

THE FOCAL POINT IN THE MAIN ROOM is the copper-clad fireplace, which grows in character as the metal ages to a rich patina. The mantel is an apple-tree trunk from an orchard in upstate New York.

PORCHES ON BOTH ENDS OF THE CABIN have deep, sheltering eaves and provide lots of outdoor space for enjoying water views and a variety of marsh wildlife.

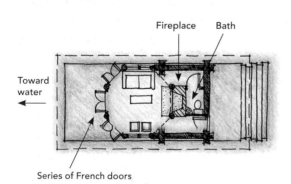

Fireplace   Bath

Toward water

Series of French doors

Scale in feet

1   6 ft.

0   3

Legacy on the Lake

BY MARIA LAPIANA

This tiny cabin sits deep in the woods of Wisconsin's Northern Highland American Legion State Forest, 220,000 pristine acres refreshed by more than 900 lakes close to the Michigan border. It's surrounded by trees, wildlife, and little else. Jerry Gunnelson built the cabin as a gift to himself, to his wife, Janet, to their children and grandchildren, and to the land itself, which he describes as "always giving and never taking."

The "council ring," a circle of stones surrounding a fire pit and a quartet of Adirondack chairs (see the photo on p. 38), invites family gatherings, campfires, and late-night conversations. Spending time at the cabin gives him peace of mind, Gunnelson says, and a sense of gratitude. "If there's one thing that gives me satisfaction," he says, "it's that there is a story here that I can pass on to my kids and grandkids."

The unassuming 400-sq.-ft. cabin is situated on a 1,100-acre chain of three fish-filled lakes. There's a single sitting room and kitchen and a sleeping loft. The windows are hinged at the top, so they can be secured when open all the way to make the cabin feel like a screened porch.

Gunnelson hired an architect to design the cabin, but he built it himself with a friend who is a car-

TUCKED IN THE WOODS, the cabin is windowed on three sides. Patio doors open to let in summer breezes and create an expansive view of the lake.

penter. They used recycled and reclaimed materials, including more than a hundred 24-ft. timbers of Douglas fir from an elementary school that had been torn down.

Because he wanted to connect the building to his roots, he brought in two oak trees from his family's farm to support the cantilevered part of the cabin. He also used stone from his father's and grandfather's farms, and even brought some back from the family's original homestead in Norway. That stone sits in the council ring.

"I knew that anything I built would detract from what nature has done, so I kept it simple," Gunnelson says.

NOTHING IS VISIBLE from the end of the pier except the lake and untouched state land.

THE CANTILEVERED FRONT of the cabin (above) rests on two oak trees felled from the owner's family farm.

THE BEDS ARE ALL BUILT IN, and the windows open upward to create a screened-porch effect.

Do-It-Yourself Retreat

BY SAMARA RAFERT

Michael and Peg, the owners of this simple dwelling, relish the peaceful views and clear weather that accompany living on the leeward side of the Olympic Mountains. They chose a rural setting between the mountains and Puget Sound and built a barnlike weekend cabin. Exposed beams, windows made from salvaged and new materials, and vintage garage doors refitted to resemble great barn sliders reflect the area's rich agricultural history.

Although they and their kids enjoy the place on summer weekends, the couple looks forward to adapting it for year-round use in retirement. "We have very good weather here in the winter," Michael says. "It's the best-kept secret." From the deck, they'll continue to enjoy views of boats in the sound, mountains changing color with the light, marsh hawks hunting in the corn fields, and thousands of stars at night.

It took a summer-long search for Michael and Peg to find their ideal piece of land, and then they ordered the makings of their 24-ft. by 32-ft. retreat from New Hampshire's Shelter-Kit, which sells easily customized kits for post-and-beam houses. Michael and some friends erected the basic structure in three weeks. To keep the interior spacious and airy, the homeowners extended the sleeping loft only partway across, creating a "great room" feel. Over the years the cabin, which sleeps 10 and frequently accommodates guests, has been modified to feel more permanent, although always clean and simple.

GO WITH THE FLOW. French doors let indoors and outdoors flow together, while exposed beams maintain the barnlike feel.

IT'S ALL ABOUT THE VIEW. The homeowners, Michael and Peg, cite the deck as their favorite aspect of the cabin. As Michael says, "Taking in the views and sipping a beer in the Adirondack chair is it."

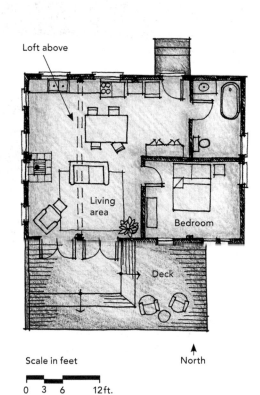

Loft above

Living area

Bedroom

Deck

Scale in feet

0   3   6   12ft.

North

KEEP IT SIMPLE. The owners emphasized simple decor throughout the small space, but bright colors and retro furnishings keep the interior lively.

Cranking Up the View

BY CHRIS ERMIDES

Overlooking a lake in northern Idaho, this contemporary cabin makes inspiring use of humble materials. Although carpenters by trade, the crew of M/C Company from Spokane, Washington, embraced the opportunity to work with concrete and steel. The cabin's most impressive feature—a 6-ton, 30-ft. by 20-ft. window that opens at the turn of a wheel—was built on-site and glazed in place. Philip Turner designed and built the window's gear-drive mechanism, which can be operated by even a young child. The cabin was designed by Tom Kundig, FAIA, of Olson Sundberg Kundig Allen Architects.

BLURRING THE LINE BETWEEN INDOORS AND OUT. When the large window is up the entire living space is open to the lake and the surrounding forest.

At Home
in the Woods

BY CHRIS ERMIDES

Though the word cabin implies rustic living, Jim Olson, a principal at Olson Sundberg Kundig Allen Architects in Seattle, proves with his version that you don't have to rough it to enjoy nature. Beginning with a 14-ft. by 14-ft. bunkhouse he built himself in 1959, Olson completed a series of three small additions and renovations over the course of 40 years. By leaving much of the structure exposed and by using subdued colors, he preserved the spare, reflective nature of a cabin. Punctuated by locally milled Douglas-fir uprights, floor-to-ceiling windows frame views of Puget Sound and Mount Rainier. A pod-like bedroom addition cleverly integrates a circular skylight well with the bed's headboard and flanking bookshelves. The simply stated cabin sits amid the lush landscape in a way that any architect or builder can appreciate. Even Thoreau would feel right at home.

BETTER THAN CAMPING. Between the skylight above and the windows on either side, sleeping in the bed is almost like sleeping in the woods, but far more comfortable.

SIMPLE LIVING. Wooden boxes that hold books and games serve as coffee tables, and the chairs would be just as comfortable outdoors as they are in.

The Crib

BY MAUREEN FRIEDMAN

A SOFT GLOW. With its translucent walls, The Crib is full of daylight without the need for windows and at night it glows from within.

Drawing inspiration from traditional farm buildings used to store corn, The Crib is architect Jeffery Broadhurst's award-winning small shelter designed to serve as a weekend cabin, a backyard office, a studio, or a guest house. The prototype (shown here) is installed at the sculpture garden at the Strathmore Arts Center in Bethesda, Maryland, and was fabricated and assembled by Enviresponsible Shelters, Rockville, Maryland, and Added Dimensions, Takoma Park, Maryland.

Broadhurst combined the concept of traditional wood timber framing with the structural simplicity of scaffolding systems to design the shop-fabricated galvanized-steel bent structure. Structural insulated panels (SIPs) supported by engineered wood and steel beams that span between the bends form the floor and roof. Prefabricated wall panels of unpainted, heat-treated poplar and translucent insulating multi-layer polycarbonate sheets are weatherstripped and clipped into the framework.

The Crib can be outfitted with a kitchen or an office, and a bathroom can be added either at the foundation level or on the main level in the larger Extended Crib model. An insulated-glass garage door opens to a deck. The Crib is factory-built using sustainable, recyclable materials, then is quickly assembled on site. To date, fabrication has been local, but Broadhurst is interested in establishing a partnership with a house fabricator/distributor with a national or international presence.

PACKING IT IN. The expandable office and sleeping loft above fit a lot of function into a tiny space. A small propanefired stainless steel fireplace and a radiant floor system heat the structure.

Chainsaw Tour de Forest

BY CHRIS ERMIDES

In the Pacific Northwest, chainsaws aren't just for felling trees and cutting firewood. They've become one of the tools most often grabbed by artists and craftsmen to create wooden sculptures. A guest cabin in a verdant British Columbia forest designed by Henry Yorke Mann unites this new tradition with Native American totem-pole traditions that are many centuries old. The project gave craftsmen at Surefit Log Homes in Chilliwack, B.C., the opportunity to display their chainsaw skills. Chainsaws were the only tools used to cut the dovetail corners on the sidewalls and to carve the arm-like supports on the totems that hold up the roof. Once cut, the supports were mortised (with a chainsaw, of course) to the white-cedar posts and secured with threaded rod. Showing off a patina of green-tinted tarnish, custom-fabricated flashing caps the ridge and protects projecting beam ends.

HEAVY-DUTY JOINERY. The exterior walls of this 400-sq.-ft. log cabin constructed by Surefit Log Homes and Trans Northern Construction are 12×12 cedar timbers that were dovetail jointed at the corners.

Cottages

A Garden Cottage for Low-Impact Living

BY NIR PEARLSON

W hen I first met my clients, Julie, a veteran elementary-school teacher, and Rob, a county commissioner, they had been living in a 600-sq.-ft. remodeled chicken coop on a 2.1-acre property for 28 years. Committed to a low-impact and highly self-sufficient lifestyle, they were on a quest to replace the chicken coop with a simple and sustainable home. Their house would need to be durable, low maintenance, and energy efficient, and it would need to complement their sprawling garden. Most of all, they hoped, their home would inspire them with beauty every day.

Julie and Rob's vision echoed my firm's mission to design sustainable small-scale homes and to promote urban infill. In addition, I immediately fell in love with their garden, an oasis of tranquility and sustenance minutes from Eugene's downtown. My firm's challenge was to design a compact house that would support a modest lifestyle yet foster a sense of abundance.

BACKYARD HOME
IN A PRIVATE SETTING

This long, narrow 2.1-acre lot hosts both a main house and the garden cottage featured here. Situated between a main thoroughfare and a greenway, the location bridges urban and natural settings.

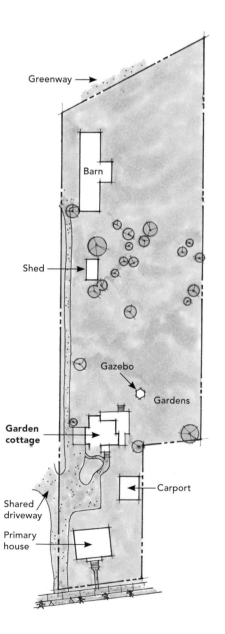

SHELTER AMID PLENTY. Decks and porches link the house to the extensive gardens surrounding it, while generous roof overhangs provide shelter from sun and rain.

A verdant site near an urban core

Julie and Rob's lot is a remnant of the farmland that surrounded Eugene in its early days, most of which has since been subdivided into small residential lots. Oriented east-west, the 700-ft.-long lot provides a generous solar exposure that combines with rich floodplain soil to make this property ideal for gardening. During the summer the vegetable garden provides most of Julie and Rob's food, as well as a surplus that they store for the winter. The lot extends between a major traffic arterial on the west and a bike path along the Willamette River to the east. Immediate access to transportation, city amenities, and the river's ecosystem translates into urban living at its very best.

In addition to its vegetable and ornamental gardens, the property hosted a weathered barn, a storage shed, Julie and Rob's chicken coop, and a bungalow from the 1920s that faces the street and is leased by long-term tenants. With no desire for large interiors, Julie and Rob had chosen to live in the smaller accessory house, and they wanted their new home to occupy the same location among the vegetable beds and fruit trees. Because they spend much of their time tending the land, maintaining visual and physical access to the outdoors was a top priority, so the design of the new house centered on the garden.

POWER AND LIGHT. In addition to shelter, the roofs provide a platform for solar panels and a venue for clerestories.

Julie and Rob wanted more space than they had in the old coop, but they were content to limit the area and height of their new home to comply with local regulations for secondary dwelling units. To accommodate future growth through greater housing density, Eugene's zoning code allows construction of accessory dwellings alongside existing homes on single-home residential properties. Although the zoning code limits the interior of an

concealed mechanical-equipment attic and an open, daylit meditation loft.

Designed for the Pacific Northwest

The Pacific Northwest is known for its long, rainy winters, prompting a "shed the water and bring in the light" strategy. Summers can be hot, however, so solar protection is necessary. Generous overhangs on the house's low-sloped shed roofs address all these issues. The south-sloping roof extends the full width of the house and shelters the great-room windows from winter storms and summer heat. It also points two solar arrays toward the sun and allows for north-facing clerestories to illuminate the guest room and loft. The north-facing roof opens the main bedroom to garden views and to mini-clerestories. A small roof on the west shelters the entry. To the south, a roof over the patio springs up and away from the house to frame expansive views and to allow low-angle winter sun to penetrate the indoors. The windows, clerestories, skylights, and three exterior glazed doors provide an ongoing connection with the outdoors and bring in ample daylight.

Julie and Rob wanted their home to represent the Pacific Northwest aesthetically as well. Combining modern forms with traditional craftsmanship, this hybrid timber-frame house includes exposed, load-bearing heavy-timber construction as well as standard joists and studs. Posts, beams, rafters, and roof decking were milled from regional Douglas fir or hemlock timber. The woodwork is clear-coated, which highlights the mineral-tinted Imperial Plaster wall finish (www.usg.com).

Sightlines and views make a small house feel spacious

Julie and Rob wanted their home to be at what they called a "human scale." Julie defines that as "not so big as to feel dwarfed and diminished, but not so small as to feel confined and limited." With Julie and Rob's human scale in mind, we designed the roof—with its rafters exposed—to define the scale, orienta-

accessory dwelling to 800 sq. ft. of living space, it allows this living space to be augmented with covered outdoor areas and storage or utility rooms with exterior access.

We took advantage of this allowance to add a mechanical room and multiple covered porches, and because areas with low headroom are not legally considered habitable rooms, we included a bonus space. This area, accessed by a ladder, includes a

tion, and character of each interior space. With no option for vast rooms, we mixed and overlapped the entry, living, dining, kitchen, and circulation spaces into a great room. Long vistas through spaces, windows, and doors foster a sense of expansion, while coves such as a window seat off the great room allow for repose.

To prevent monotony, spaces are delineated by changes in flooring or with cabinets or built-ins. For example, the slate flooring transitions from the entry into a simple hearth, where a woodstove visually anchors the great room.

Third-party certification confirms the home's quality construction

Julie and Rob's commitment to sustainable living allowed us to select strategies to reduce their carbon footprint significantly. This earned their home an Earth Advantage Platinum Certification, the highest level offered by Earth Advantage New Homes, an Oregon-based third-party certification program. Earth Advantage weighs energy efficiency, indoor-air quality, resource efficiency, environmental responsibility, and water conservation.

The roof and walls were sheathed with a continuous layer of rigid foam, 1 in. on the walls and 2 in. on the roof. This foam prevents thermal bridging and insulates well beyond code levels. Daylight from the windows minimizes the need for electric lighting, and a minisplit heat pump couples with a heat-recovery ventilator to heat and ventilate the home efficiently. A woodstove provides backup heat and ambience.

A grid-tied solar photovoltaic array offsets summertime electricity use; domestic hot water is provided by a solar hot-water collector. In the future, a gray-water diversion system and rainwater catchment cisterns will supply irrigation water to the gardens.

DURABLE DETAILS

LONG-LASTING EXTERIOR FINISHES are a big part of sustainable building, and the Pacific Northwest's damp climate can be unforgiving to poorly detailed exteriors. Low-maintenance finishes include copper-penny metal roofing, fascia cladding, gutters, and downspouts. The steel columns are painted to complement the roof. Most of the building is clad with fiber cement lap siding. This durable, low-maintenance material is simple to install, and it provides a familiar, homey look. Wall areas that are protected by eaves or by patio roofs feature stained plywood. Similarly, the Douglas fir exterior doors are protected by overhanging roofs. The windows are wood with aluminum cladding.

DAYLIGHT, NOT CABINETS. Windows bring light and space to the work areas. Storage cabinets cluster on interior walls.

Julie and Rob are satisfied with their new home. Julie says, "Our home is the intimate interplay of inside cozy places of sanctuary and outside gardens splashing light and life through windows. The eye and heart dance from one angle of beauty to another as the intersections create a peaceful harmony."

DELINEATED BY FUNCTION. A peninsula with barstool seating defines the kitchen, while a stove hearth and window seat invite relaxation in the great room. A small altar marks the entrance to the main bedroom.

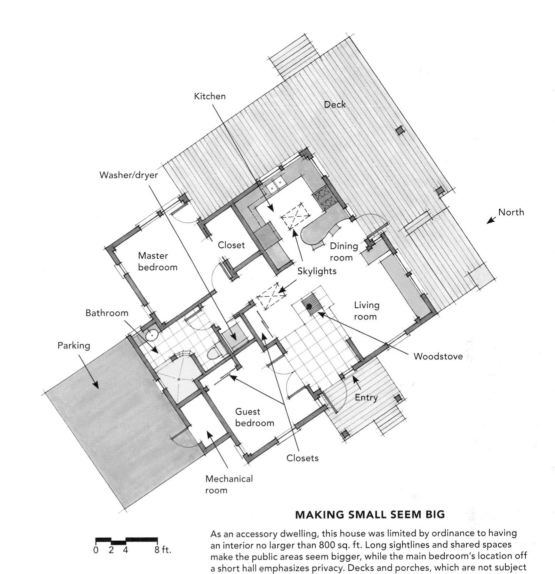

Kitchen

Deck

Washer/dryer

North

Closet

Dining room

Master bedroom

Skylights

Bathroom

Living room

Parking

Woodstove

Entry

Guest bedroom

Closets

Mechanical room

0 2 4 8 ft.

MAKING SMALL SEEM BIG

As an accessory dwelling, this house was limited by ordinance to having an interior no larger than 800 sq. ft. Long sightlines and shared spaces make the public areas seem bigger, while the main bedroom's location off a short hall emphasizes privacy. Decks and porches, which are not subject to the same size restrictions, were used to expand the house both visually and physically. Carefully placed doors and windows provide access to these decks and porches, as well as to the extensive gardens.

SPECS

Bedrooms: 2
Bathrooms: 1
Size: 800 sq. ft.
Cost: $270 per sq. ft.
Completed: 2012
Location: Eugene, Oregon
Architect: Nir Pearlson Architect; www.green-building.com
Builder: Six Degrees Construction; www.sixdegreesconstruction.com

The Second Time Around

BY CHARLES BICKFORD

The tiny house wasn't that old, but it was failing fast. Built in 1950 by an industrial arts class at Martha's Vineyard High School, the house sat on a depression that didn't drain; consequently, it was rotting away. It was a tough situation for Ellen Epstein, who bought the house in the 1970s as a three-season getaway. When she wasn't there, she shared the house with seven families of old friends, and everyone loved the place. But despite a community effort toward the upkeep and maintenance, saving the structure was a losing battle.

Ellen decided to demolish the house; then she hired the local South Mountain Co. to design and build a new house that could be used year-round. Because of the small lot's setbacks, the house had to remain in the same footprint, so the primary challenge for the design/build firm was to keep the house small and in scale with the neighborhood, but to increase the amenities and living space. The project also marked the first time that South Mountain designer Laurel Wilkinson and foreman Aaron Beck took a new-home project from start to finish.

COMPACT AND CHARMING. Built on the footprint of a failing three-season house (right), the new 1,000-sq.-ft. home is both energy and space efficient. Photo on the facing page taken at A on floor plan.

How do you make more room in the same space?

At 625 sq. ft., the original house was euphemistically cozy, realistically too small. The new design called for at least two bedrooms, two baths, and enough storage space for each of the seven families and all their books. The big answer to the quandary was to add a second floor. This extra 400 sq. ft. allowed for a multi-use loft/family room, a half-bathroom, a quiet upstairs bedroom, several closets, and a built-in desk. In turn, the first-floor areas became more spacious, with a larger bedroom, a full bath, and dining, kitchen, and living areas. Wilkinson used

BEFORE

FOUR SPACE-SAVING FEATURES FOR A SMALL FLOOR PLAN

1. **The most useful mudroom possible.** Use built-ins to stop clutter at the entry.

2. **Double-duty built-ins.** A bookcase stores the family favorites where a half-wall was needed anyway.

3. **Light-filled loft.** At the top of the stairs, an open loft is another place for family members to get away.

4. **An outside alternative.** An alfresco shower works for this family almost year-round and is a good example of how to use space.

SPECS

Bedrooms: 2
Bathrooms: 1½
Size: 1,018 sq. ft.
Insulation: R-29 (walls); R-49 (roof)
Location: Vineyard Haven, Massachusetts
Architect/builder: South Mountain Co. (Laurel Wilkinson, lead designer; Aaron Beck, lead carpenter)

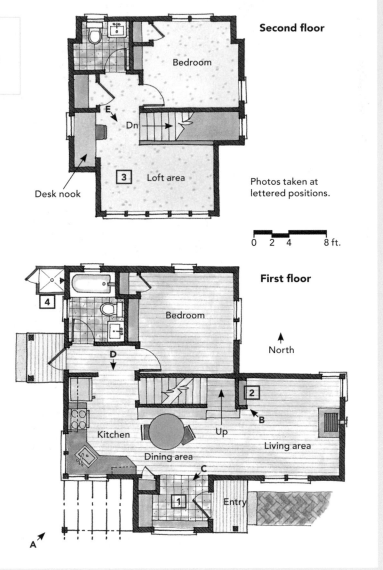

Second floor

Bedroom

E

Dn

3 Loft area

Desk nook

Photos taken at lettered positions.

0 2 4   8 ft.

First floor

4

Bedroom

North

D

2

B

Kitchen   Up   Living area

Dining area

C

1   Entry

A

the footprint space that was previously occupied by a porch to make a 50-sq.-ft. mudroom at the entrance, which became Ellen's favorite room.

Of course, there was a lot more to saving space than just cutting up the floor plan. Built-in bookcases, shelves, benches, and a desk all were fitted into available space. Because the house is used primarily in the warmer months, the second shower is outside, a local tradition that doesn't require the use of floor space inside.

A tight envelope keeps down energy costs

Ellen had hoped that her new house's energy requirements could be satisfied with solar power. Unfortunately, a large oak tree stood between the house and solar gain. The tree's importance to the lot was greater than that of the photovoltaic panels. That didn't mean Ellen couldn't have an efficient house. The builders first air-sealed and insulated the frame. Triple-glazed windows from Loewen® helped

THE BEST ROOM IN THE HOUSE. Built in place of the former enclosed porch, the mudroom's tile floor and well-ordered storage keep the rest of the house free of sand, dirt, and outerwear. Double skylights and windows brighten the 50-sq.-ft. space. Photo taken at C on floor plan.

THE BEST ROOM IN THE HOUSE. Built in place of the former enclosed porch, the mudroom's tile floor and well-ordered storage keep the rest of the house free of sand, dirt, and outerwear. Double skylights and windows brighten the 50-sq.-ft. space. Photo taken at C on floor plan.

INNOVATIVE SPACE. In the living area, a bookshelf that doubles as a stair rail and a stair tread that continues as a built-in bench are two strategies to conserve space. Photo taken at B on floor plan.

to keep the overall R-value high. Blower-door tests were performed three times, yielding a final reading several times tighter than code.

On the demand side, daylighting strategies and energy-efficient appliances and lighting fixtures were used to lighten the house's load. Because the house is built to be so tight, a point-source propane heater by Jøtul® in the living room is all that's needed to heat the structure. Enerjoy® electric radiant panels (www.sshcinc.com) mounted in the bedroom ceilings also were added as a backup for cold winter nights.

Blending in with the neighborhood

The house sits on a tiny road and occupies the centermost of three small lots. The exterior is sided with white-cedar shingles and trimmed in reclaimed cypress, all of which will be allowed to weather. Against that traditional backdrop, the builders added a few details that created a great deal of charm without a lot of expense. The unusual muntin arrangement in the windows is a South Mountain trademark of sorts, and here it was offered without an extra charge by the window manufacturer. A simple trellis screens the entry, and a pergola provides a shady spot for sitting outdoors.

THE MULTIFUNCTION LOFT. At the top of the stairs, a bright and open room serves as a family room, study, or spare bedroom as the occasion dictates. Separated from the stairs by only a kneewall, the room feels much bigger than its dimensions would indicate. Photo taken at E on floor plan.

INFORMALITY SUITS THIS KITCHEN. Made of reclaimed cypress, the open shelves and cabinets make efficient, accessible storage. Larger items are stored on the continuous shelf that runs across the tops of the cabinets. Photo taken at D on floor plan.

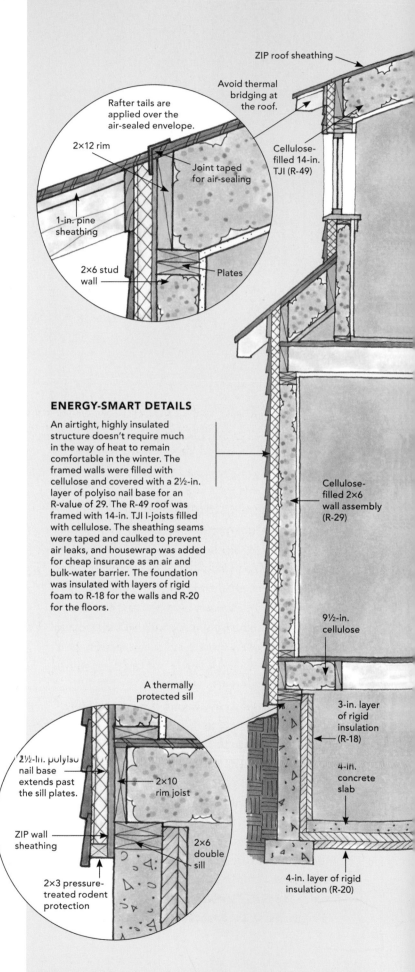

Rafter tails are applied over the air-sealed envelope.

2×12 rim

Joint taped for air-sealing

1-in. pine sheathing

2×6 stud wall

Plates

ZIP roof sheathing

Avoid thermal bridging at the roof.

Cellulose-filled 14-in. TJI (R-49)

ENERGY-SMART DETAILS

An airtight, highly insulated structure doesn't require much in the way of heat to remain comfortable in the winter. The framed walls were filled with cellulose and covered with a 2½-in. layer of polyiso nail base for an R-value of 29. The R-49 roof was framed with 14-in. TJI I-joists filled with cellulose. The sheathing seams were taped and caulked to prevent air leaks, and housewrap was added for cheap insurance as an air and bulk-water barrier. The foundation was insulated with layers of rigid foam to R-18 for the walls and R-20 for the floors.

Cellulose-filled 2×6 wall assembly (R-29)

9½-in. cellulose

A thermally protected sill

2½-in. polyiso nail base extends past the sill plates.

ZIP wall sheathing

2×3 pressure-treated rodent protection

2×10 rim joist

2×6 double sill

3-in. layer of rigid insulation (R-18)

4-in. concrete slab

4-in. layer of rigid insulation (R-20)

Small Cottage Makes a Big Splash

BY DAVID EVANS

SLOPING TOWARD THE VIEWS. A 12-ft.-tall walk-out basement puts the main floor high enough to enjoy the panoramic views of Puget Sound.

A professor in architecture school once told me that good design often is measured by what's not there. This project started out as a guesthouse for a much grander master plan. Instead, it evolved into a simpler solution and became an exercise in seeking delight in the minimal and in keeping down the scale to emphasize the detail.

A tall basement for a steep lot

Located in a small historic town on Puget Sound in Washington, this house was to be a second home for my wife and me, with hopes that it would become our permanent dwelling. After a long search we found a site with many wonderful features—along with some daunting challenges.

The corner lot in an old neighborhood had been overgrown and neglected for years. But it was blessed with panoramic views of the Sound over the neighbors' rooftops. More thorny issues were that the lot sat next to a major crosstown street with a fair bit of traffic noise and that the site sloped steeply downhill toward the views.

To maximize the views, we located the house in the highest corner of the lot. I oriented the long dimension of the house in the direction of the slope, which maximized solar gain. Unfortunately, though, the grade in this corner sloped 14 ft. over the length

THE LOW-MAINTENANCE STUCCO EXTERIOR was applied directly over walls of concrete and foam. Photo taken at A on floor plan.

of the house. The city required that auto access be from the side street, which put the driveway and garage on the lowest part of the lot. A 12-ft.-tall foundation houses the garage and walk-out basement, and it places the main floor of the house at the right level for the upper grade of the lot.

A house of small additions

I put the entrance on the main level where it would relate better to the street. Boosted by the tall basement, the public spaces on this level now look out over the neighboring rooftops to the Sound. How-

ever, a third floor above the main level would have grown the building to over 34 ft. from the lowest floor to the peak of its 15-in-12 pitch roof. Rather than present such a tall façade to the street, I decided to make the house a story-and-a-half tall. This height gives the house better proportions and makes the loft level feel like a converted attic.

To blend in the house with the established neighborhood, I used antique materials and designed the house to look like it had been added on to over time. I started with a simple rectangular footprint. A small bump-out addition to the south houses a

GOING UP INSTEAD OF OUT. The public spaces on the main level are blessed with views of Puget Sound. The house's story-and-a-half design makes the upper level feel like a converted attic.

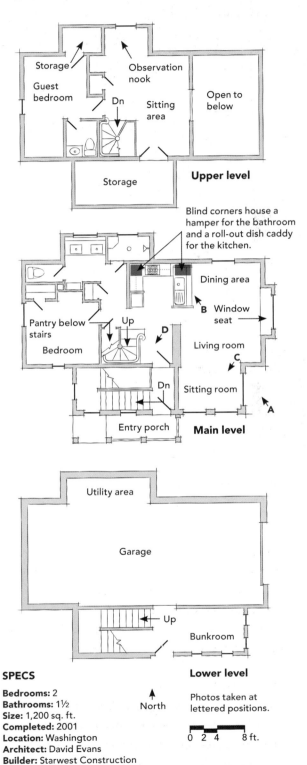

STACKED AND COMPACT

To make use of a small footprint, this house stacks two floors on top of a tall walk-out basement. The lower level houses the garage and utilities as well as a small auxiliary bunkroom.

Storage
Guest bedroom
Observation nook
Dn
Sitting area
Open to below
Storage
Upper level

Blind corners house a hamper for the bathroom and a roll-out dish caddy for the kitchen.

Dining area
B Window seat
Pantry below stairs
Up
D
Living room
Bedroom
C
Dn
Sitting room
A
Entry porch
Main level

Utility area
Garage
Up
Bunkroom
Lower level

SPECS

Bedrooms: 2
Bathrooms: 1½
Size: 1,200 sq. ft.
Completed: 2001
Location: Washington
Architect: David Evans
Builder: Starwest Construction

North

Photos taken at lettered positions.

0 2 4   8 ft.

stairwell, with a lower entry and bunkroom on the garage level. On the main level this addition expands to include a lean-to entry porch, the entrance vestibule, and a sunny sitting room off the living room.

Another addition on the north side helps to break up the tall and unrelieved elevation (see the photo above). This dormered addition makes space for a utility area in the garage; a large, compartmentalized main-floor bathroom; and an observation nook on the upper level.

ICF walls address seismic concerns

Building tall and narrow in the northwestern part of the country always raises seismic red flags. A wall system of insulated-concrete forms (ICFs) deals with this issue. This system is very strong and resistant to earth movements. But strength is just the beginning.

In the extreme coastal environment, rot and deterioration due to weather are a constant worry. The insulated-concrete wall system eliminates wood in the exterior walls. We veneered the outside of the ICFs with bluestone to lend visual weight to the lower level. Integrally colored stucco applied directly

to the insulated forms gives the rest of the walls a durable low-maintenance finish. The walls also even out interior temperature swings between day and night. As a side benefit, the thick walls also help to mitigate street noise.

I chose steel-sash windows for their low maintenance. Instead of wood trim, we beveled the edges of the forms around the window and door openings to create stucco returns on the outside and plaster returns inside. The only trim pieces are the heavy bluestone sills inside and out for each window.

Recycled Roof Completes the Cottage Look

I wanted a roof as low-maintenance as the exterior of the house. Authentic Roof (www.authenticroof.com), a recycled rubber product, looks like slate but is much easier to install and costs much less. I capped the ridges with clay tiles from Great Britain.

The exposed rafter tails actually are 4-ft.-long pieces of 3×5 cedar spliced onto the conventional 2×10 rafters and evenly spaced across the eaves. Fir 2×4s finish the exposed roof deck. The rafter tails were set at a lower pitch to give the roof a more relaxed look at the edges.

The cottage appearance is enhanced by the large half-round zinc gutters and downspouts. The eave and rake trim, along with the oversize gable vents, are made of cedar in a simple Asian pattern.

Living Compact

Living in the confines of a small house is appealing because, by design, it creates a feeling of closeness and intimacy. The galley kitchen opens into the dining and living areas to enhance the spatial flow while reinforcing a sense of community in the house.

In a more controversial move, the house is equipped with only one full bathroom. But to make that bath accommodate two people at once, the shower and toilet each have their own separate compartments. Two sinks allow for simultaneous grooming as well.

A DRIVEWAY THAT YOU MOW

WITH OUR HOUSE sitting at the top of the slope, the city was concerned about runoff ending up in the neighbor's lot downhill. Our solution was a product called Grasspave2 (www.invisiblestructures.com), which produces a drivable grown-in turf surface. We literally turned our lawn into a driveway and parking area.

Grasspave2 is a porous paving system that creates enough load-bearing capacity for a large vehicle while providing a medium for growing grass without compaction. The key ingredient is a ring-and-grid mat that sits on a layer of gravel and sand. The mat comes as square-meter or quarter-meter sections assembled into rolls. The mat is filled with sand for proper drainage, and grass grows in the sand. Surface water drains to the middle of the site via perforated drainpipe. The lawn we planted obscures the mat. The rest of the yard was seeded with a wildflower mix for a low-maintenance natural look.

Despite its size, the main floor boasts many different places to settle. In addition to the living- and dining-room areas, an arched opening leads into a sunny sitting room. A built-in seat in front of the tall arch-top window is the perfect spot to relax and watch the sailboats on the Sound in the distance.

We paid special attention to maximizing the storage in our limited space. The kitchen is a perfect example. We chose compact appliances and a low-profile retractable range hood that use a minimum amount of space. To solve the blind-corner cabinet problem, I designed a dish-storage

TINY BUT FUNCTIONAL. Although tiny in area, this galley uses space judiciously to create a full working kitchen. In addition to other space-saving appliances, the narrow-profile range hood switches on when it's extended.

EVERY CORNER PUT TO USE. A dish caddy that lives in the blind corner of the peninsula rolls over to the small but roomy dishwasher for quick unloading. The other blind corner is home to a hamper that opens to the bathroom.

TAKING THE GALLEY OUT OF THE KITCHEN. A curved soffit and an angular peninsula open the kitchen into the dining area to make it seem larger. Photo taken at B on floor plan.

caddy that can be wheeled to the dishwasher. The other blind corner becomes a pullout hamper that is next to the bathroom.

A showcase for fine craftsmanship

Inside the main entry, all of the major interior materials are introduced in the vestibule: creamy yellow hand-troweled plaster, mahogany, yellow cedar, and Douglas fir. This simple palette is repeated throughout the house to unify the compact spaces and to call out special elements crafted by local artisans.

The custom cabinetry in the kitchen and bathroom features simple mahogany frames with flat Douglas-fir panels. A dramatic curved soffit above the kitchen peninsula ushers the eye into the vertical expanse of the living and dining room. A surprising periwinkle-blue Italian plaster ceiling carries down onto the walls in a playful, undulating pattern. To enhance the drama, the outer face of the kitchen peninsula and a thick battered wall adjacent to the kitchen angle as if leaning into the living and dining room.

From the main entry, a heavy mahogany and fir door leads to an artful staircase that winds to the upper level. Conceived of more as a piece of cabinetry than as a staircase, the project resulted from a long collaboration between local woodworker Gaylen Marrs and me. Infill panels around a pantry closet feature a carved tableau of a local coastal pine. The wood details are complemented by an exuberant wrought-iron railing that was hand-forged by local blacksmith Steve Lopes. A sinuous mahogany handrail slithers from the iron volute below to the gooseneck at the top. Marrs carved the top of the newel at the center of the stair to mimic a deconstructed log.

STAIRS AS ART. (left) The centerpiece for the fine craftsmanship in this house is the stairway to the upper level. A tree carved in relief grows out of the stair skirt and wraps around a small closet pantry. Photo taken at D on floor plan.

THE NEWEL CONTINUES THE THEME. (above left and right) The center newel is carved to look like a tree trunk breaking down. A serpentine mahogany railing caps off the wrought-iron balustrade and then winds its way to the upper level.

A Higher Standard

BY JESSE THOMPSON

For a number of years, Rob and Fiona were content to live in a simple Maine cottage a stone's throw from the water's edge. In recent years, however, they had tried having a new house designed to accommodate their changing needs, but quickly got mired in results that were much larger and more expensive than what they wanted. After tiring of these unsuccessful ventures, they came to my firm seeking a compact, modern, extremely energy-efficient home that would blend into the tightly woven neighborhood where they planned to root themselves for the years to come.

We set to work applying our studio's motto—beautiful, sustainable, attainable—to the project. Our early meetings quickly centered on the meaning of cottage in the 21st century. We wondered if the term still defined the classic British buildings of Rob and Fiona's youth, which so successfully fit between clusters of lavender and privet hedges, or if cottage had come to mean something bolder and simpler with less of the romantic touchstones of 19th-century construction. We concluded that we needed to draw on each of these ideas, and that the house would need to be simple, tough, and practical, in keeping with the Maine life that Rob and Fiona love.

We thought that a house approximately 1,800 sq. ft. in size would be able to meet their budget and allow for the quality of design and construction they desired. Early on it became evident that their goals included very low energy use, nontoxic materials, a quiet and simple aesthetic, bedrooms that faced the water, a flexible office space, and LEED certification.

Ultimately, we designed a house that met all those wishes. The house feels spacious and comfortable, it's certified LEED Platinum, it beats the Passive House airtightness standard by 30 percent, and it meets the Architecture 2030 Challenge of reducing fossil-fuel use by 70 percent when measured against average homes in the region. Although we were able to accomplish all of this for only $175 per sq. ft., we had to navigate plenty of challenges along the way to make the project a reality.

MAKING THE MOST OF THE SITE. The home's back rises dramatically to capture light and views.

The site dictates form and layout

Rob and Fiona's site was challenging. The outstanding views on the property are to the west. However, the axis of the Flying Point Peninsula on which the house sits stretches from northeast to southwest, and solar south didn't align with either direction.

We generated a variety of sketches to test the best house position. The most comfortable scheme locked the main axis of the house perpendicular to the road, which is typical of homes in the neighborhood, but we twisted the interior views along the diagonal and placed large corner windows in all important rooms. We also pushed the prime rooms toward the back of the house as close to the water as we could, letting the house rise up in a simple wedge shape to cover the spaces inside. This provided interior rooms with stunning ocean views and allowed us to chase as much southern exposure for the triple-glazed windows as we could, exposing the slab to as much free heat as possible.

The resulting house shape feels quiet and centered, and the approach to the structure provides a gradual introduction to the home. A modest gabled porch connects to a timber-frame carport and presents a welcoming entry, not unlike the many cottages on this part of the coast.

High-stakes, straightforward construction

Our design methodology revolves around marrying a smart building shell to as small and affordable a mechanical system as we can specify. This building site had several fuel options available: electricity, propane, oil, and wood. We haven't installed an oil boiler in a house in many years because we think

First floor

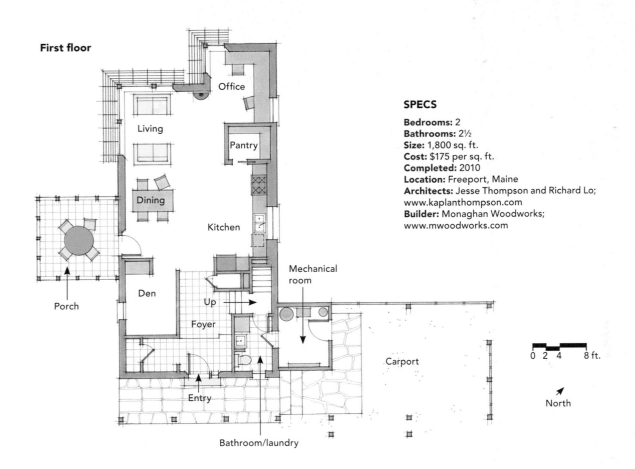

Office

Living

Pantry

Dining

Kitchen

Porch

Den

Up

Foyer

Mechanical room

Entry

Carport

Bathroom/laundry

0 2 4 8 ft.

North

SPECS

Bedrooms: 2
Bathrooms: 2½
Size: 1,800 sq. ft.
Cost: $175 per sq. ft.
Completed: 2010
Location: Freeport, Maine
Architects: Jesse Thompson and Richard Lo;
www.kaplanthompson.com
Builder: Monaghan Woodworks;
www.mwoodworks.com

Second floor

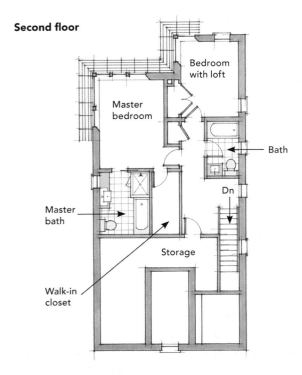

Bedroom with loft

Master bedroom

Bath

Master bath

Dn

Storage

Walk-in closet

that it's far too toxic and inefficient to store 275 gal. of hydrocarbons inside a modern building. Also, a masonry chimney had no place in the project for other reasons. Rob and Fiona didn't want air conditioning, so a major advantage of heat pumps would have been wasted on the project. Therefore, we designed the house around a simple, single-zone propane-fired in-slab radiant-heating system, with the help of a flat-plate solar system designed to produce 60 percent of the likely hot-water needs of the family. By keeping complicated mixing valves, pumps, and controls out of the project, we were able to free a substantial amount of money to improve the quality of the building shell without raising construction costs. This was significant because such a simple mechanical system wouldn't work without a tough, warm building surrounding it.

We worked closely with the builder to evaluate various costs and construction methods for the walls and roof. The most economical method proved

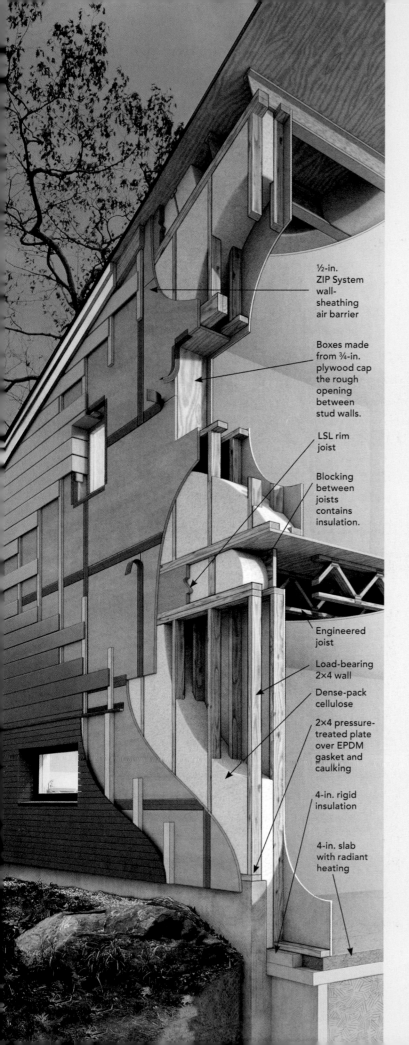

½-in. ZIP System wall-sheathing air barrier

Boxes made from ¾-in. plywood cap the rough opening between stud walls.

LSL rim joist

Blocking between joists contains insulation.

Engineered joist

Load-bearing 2×4 wall

Dense-pack cellulose

2×4 pressure-treated plate over EPDM gasket and caulking

4-in. rigid insulation

4-in. slab with radiant heating

NINE DETAILS OF A HIGH-PERFORMANCE DESIGN

1. A heavily insulated concrete slab-on-grade foundation eliminates the need for deep excavation below the high-water line, sump pumps that can fail, expensive basement insulation, and the accompanying drywall.

2. An initial design with 12-in.-thick walls yields a well-insulated assembly. It's always easier to thin up walls if necessary to gain space later in the planning stage than to have to go in the other direction.

3. A high-quality, well-sealed, and verified building shell is a must. Careful flashing details and rigorous air-sealing measures are verified with multiple blower-door tests throughout construction.

4. A house should breathe through a set of lungs, not by hoping that fresh air will somehow find its way inside. A high-quality ventilation system with heat recovery ensures health and efficiency.

5. An exterior air barrier comprised of ZIP System® wall sheathing with taped seams is the easiest to build. A simple house form with overhangs and other details added after taping the basic box made hitting 0.4 ACH50 possible.

6. Self-adhesive flashing membranes stick poorly to ZIP sheathing. Flashing membranes should be stuck onto the ZIP tape that has been applied to the sheathing.

7. Spray foam around windows leaks. Water moves through pinhole "folds" in the foam at the rough openings. Caulking the spray foam to stop leakage around the windows is necessary.

8. Concrete slabs leak air far more than expected. Air moves through the crushed-stone layer, right through the insulation gap at the slab edge and into the conditioned space. It takes a considerable amount of tape and caulk to seal this transition.

9. You don't need spray-foam insulation and/or airtight drywall for rigorous air-sealing. A sheathing air barrier, tape, and caulk do this well.

to be double 2×4 walls with an exterior air barrier, dense-packed with cellulose insulation. The roof was framed with 14-in. I-joists also dense-packed with cellulose. Our insulating target was based on a 5-20-40-60 building enclosure as laid out by Building Science Corp. for our climate zone: R-5 windows, R-20 underslab insulation, R 40 walls, and R-60 roof.

Our approach to the house's assembly, though not revolutionary, was proven extraordinary when the mechanical-sub bids came back. We went out for three bids. One price was more than $30,000 and added staple-up radiant tubing under the entire second floor in addition to our specified equipment. Another came back with a handwritten note declining to bid because the contractor had never seen such low heat loads and didn't believe they were possible to achieve. The final bid came in from a contractor who trusted our heat-loss calculations and bid $15,000. The $15,000 we saved paid for all the upgrades of insulation and for the triple-glazing in the windows.

Triple-glazed windows typically eat up a significant portion of a construction budget, so we carefully consider the units we use. For this house, we chose InLine Fiberglass windows out of Toronto. These windows were well priced compared to similar products, the fiberglass exterior was ideal for a tough waterfront location, they were available with high solar-heat gain Cardinal 179 glazing, and they had great design-pressure values to prevent water infiltration and air leakage. The windows are a combination of fixed, casement, and awning units. Using large fixed lites in combination with smaller operable units is the most economical way to get large windows into a low-budget project.

None of these design efforts would have been worthwhile, however, if the house wasn't built to be airtight. The contracting firm on the project had built many nice homes and had years of experience with coastal construction. This was their first LEED project, however, as well as their first project targeting an ambitious air-sealing specification. They teamed up with a high-quality local cellulose con-

tractor who brought his blower door on site as soon as the ZIP System sheathing shell was in place and the windows were installed. They carefully swept over the entire building skin before any insulation showed up on the project, and took our 1.0 ACH50 specification as a challenge to be crushed. After we told them that the hardest metric to hit was the Passive House standard of 0.6 ACH50, they raised their game even further. The final blower-door number, taken when the house was complete, came back at 0.4 ACH50, with less than 150 cfm50 moving through the fan under pressure.

Giving the house lungs

The goal of the mechanical system was to keep it simple and low cost. To ensure that this was possible, we carefully integrated the HRV system into the construction system. We laid out all the interior ductwork in consultation with the ventilation contractor, checking for clashes throughout the 3D

CAPTURING THE SUN'S ENERGY. The windows are oriented to enable valuable daylight to heat the house passively during Maine's notoriously cold winters.

CAD model with framing members or vertical elements. We specified open-web floor joists to allow easy mechanical, plumbing, and electrical coordination in a house with no attic or basement. Adding a few dropped ceilings gave us extra room for mechanical runs in certain areas.

Efficiency complemented by coast-appropriate finishes

The Maine coast can be a brutal environment to live and work in. Just like the people who live in them, the homes here experience some of the most severe weather conditions in the country. Wind and water come from all directions, and leaky windows and walls provide regular tales of woe from local contractors and homeowners up and down the coast. Houses here need to be built with resilient materials. Rob and Fiona also wanted to use as many local, renewable, and nontoxic materials in their home's construction as possible. Our contractor kept a close watch to ensure that highly off-gassing sealants didn't creep onto the job site, and we worked hard to make sure that no sheet goods containing urea formaldehyde or other noxious products ended up

CAPTURING THE VIEW. Contemporary interior spaces are arranged at the back of the house, adjacent to large corner windows that provide water views in the most-often-used spaces.

in the building. The flooring was a simple palette of polished concrete and carbonized bamboo with water-based polyurethane, both of which are incredibly durable. We used local lumber for all the framing and the exposed exterior woodwork, primarily hemlock and white cedar.

The siding is factory-finished fiber cement, which we applied on the flat over furring strips. We used standard smooth fiber-cement clapboards for the upper siding section on 1×3 furring strips, and fiber-cement battens on 2×4 furring strips on the lower section for added visual depth at the base of the house. In addition, the contractor upgraded the window sill pans and horizontal flashings to copper for true 100-year durability and a more elegant look.

This house is a proud moment in the history of our firm. We worked to bring a fine grain of detailing to the durable, low-energy construction techniques we have deployed on previous projects at the same time that we managed to evoke the serene modernism that our clients love. That feels like success to us.

Carriage-House Comeback

BY MATT HUTCHINS

In Seattle, several small houses are popping up, but they are not where you might expect. Modeled on carriage houses of old, these backyard cottages are second houses on the same lots as primary residences. They offer occupants established, walkable neighborhoods, with the public transportation and local businesses sorely lacking in far-flung suburbs.

To keep the cottages in sync with neighborhood character, Seattle's new zoning ordinance is strict: In addition to conforming to typical total lot coverage, setbacks, and off-street parking, a cottage can be no more than 800 net sq. ft., with a 23-ft. height limit. The net-square-footage rule means that the thickness of the walls is not included in the total amount of living space.

Our firm, CAST architecture, was itching to design a house that would satisfy the city's new rules and whatever needs a client might bring to the party. Enter Ken and Marilyn Widner. They had been thinking about downsizing after retirement, and having a new cottage seemed like the perfect solution to update their lifestyle without having to leave their beloved neighborhood. Instead of spending time cleaning the 3,000-sq.-ft. house they raised their family in, they would be able to rent it and spend time traveling.

Their goals didn't stop there. The Widners wanted to keep as much yard as possible for gardening, to build green, to harvest rainwater, and to make space for their vinyl LP collection and mementos collected from a lifetime of travel. The new house also had to be a good neighbor to the turn-of-the-20th-century bungalows lining the street.

We sat down with the site map, subtracted the setbacks, and calculated the available lot coverage. The maximum buildable footprint was 452 sq. ft. With a two-story house, we were in business.

Compromises and a comfortable kitchen

Not everything magically fits into a smaller footprint. At our first meeting we sketched out the basics: a two-bedroom house with 1½ baths. Some choices were easy, such as skipping a formal dining

OUTDOOR ROOMS MAKE SMALL HOUSES LARGER. A dining table and chairs extend the living space to the garden. Buried beneath the patio, a 1,500-gal. cistern stores runoff for toilets, laundry, and irrigation. The steeply pitched gable roof echoes those of neighboring houses. Photo taken at A on floor plan.

NO WASTED SPACE

Locating storage, stairs, and the radiant-floor boiler closet on the west wall allowed plenty of windows on the east wall. The kitchen has lots of counter space, but not much floor space, which encourages guests to stay on the dining-table side of the peninsula.

First floor

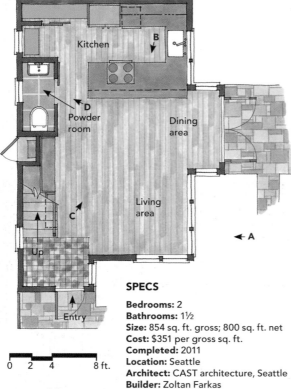

0   2   4   8 ft.

SPECS

Bedrooms: 2
Bathrooms: 1½
Size: 854 sq. ft. gross; 800 sq. ft. net
Cost: $351 per gross sq. ft.
Completed: 2011
Location: Seattle
Architect: CAST architecture, Seattle
Builder: Zoltan Farkas

Second floor

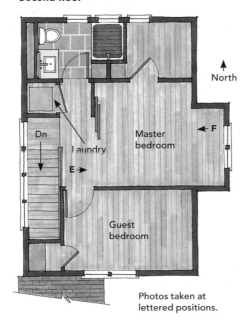

North

Photos taken at lettered positions.

room; summertime dining in the garden would take its place. In the entry, we opted for a coatrack instead of a closet. Upstairs, a stackable washer/dryer coupled with a big linen closet eliminated the need for a laundry room. Other decisions were tough; for example, the cottage doesn't have a tub, much to Marilyn's chagrin.

Marilyn does a lot of cooking and baking. She needed a big work counter with space around the stove and ample cabinets, but she didn't need floor area for multiple cooks. We pored through every drawer in her original kitchen to learn what Marilyn needed space for in her new kitchen. Now Marilyn is never more than a few steps from every dish, spatula, and cookie sheet, and she still has plenty of room for her giant paella pan.

FOCUS ON THE GARDEN. (facing page) Clustering storage, stairs, and the powder room along the west wall allowed plenty of east-facing windows overlooking the garden. The big peninsula is cooking central, with a bar, space for buffets, dish storage, and glass display. A slightly lower ceiling on the west side of the living room is a subtle suggestion of the path through the house. Photo taken at C on floor plan.

FUN WITH COLOR. Rubicund walls in the powder room add a sumptuous backdrop for an antique mirror and a retro bucket sink. The porthole reflected in the mirror is over the commode. Photo taken at D on floor plan.

NO DOWNSTAIRS PARTI-TIONS. Long diagonal views from the kitchen to the entry stretch the sense of space. The tansu-style staircase packs a lot of storage into a small space. Like the floor, the tansu unit is made of engineered bamboo. Photo taken at B on floor plan.

INHABIT THE ROOF.
The vaulted ceilings
and window bump-out
in the master bedroom
heighten the sense of
space. Barn doors close
off the room for privacy
when guests are in town.
Photos taken at F and E
on floor plan.

Cathedral ceilings and long views energize the house

Vaulting a ceiling can make all the difference between drab and dramatic. Upstairs, we vaulted all the ceilings and placed skylights in every room and in the walk-in closet. Seattle's gray winter skies are actually filled with bright, even light—enough to keep the lights off. In the bathroom the light streaming from above bounces off the azure glass tiles, giving the whole room a sun-kissed Mediterranean feel.

To make the cottage feel big, we ganged the closed functions (storage, cabinets, bathrooms, utilities) and pushed them to the north and west walls, where windows would have been facing neighboring houses. The staircase became a tansu cabinet housing the stereo, LPs, flat-screen TV, books, and mementos. Behind the TV, a boiler for the hydronic radiant floors is accessed from outside. This left a relatively large area with great light on the east and south overlooking the garden. A room with a view will always feel bigger than it is.

A year later

The Widners' cottage has been the talk of the neighborhood—not because of its size, but because of how it feels large and cozy at the same time. When we hosted an open house for the public last July, one person commented in disbelief, "800 square feet? It feels like twice that." Having lived in the house for a year now, Ken and Marilyn wouldn't want all that extra space anyway.

FOCUS ON DETAILS

Details breathe life into a house. By having less square footage, the Widners could concentrate on better materials and fixtures. Here are some highlights:

- Custom cherry cabinetry
- Custom metal railings with stainless-steel cable rail
- Premium double-hung windows from Marvin® and portholes from Andersen®
- Copper gutter and rain chain
- Vertical-grain Douglas-fir trim and doors
- Glass tile in the master bath
- An antique mirror and powder-room retro bucket sink from Alape®
- A custom pot rack made of the rock screen used by quarries to separate gravel
- A laminated bamboo handrail that resembles custom inlay, which is simply two layers of Plyboo®
- Radiant floors (concrete downstairs, Warmboard® upstairs)

A Pocket-Size House That Lives Large

BY TIMOTHY GORDON

Evening is the best time to arrive at Leslie Gordon's house on the Oregon coast. The driveway cuts through a dense swath of spruce forest. At the crest of the hill it opens to a clearing, revealing a sheltered cluster of hip-roofed buildings surrounded by a stone-walled garden. As you step onto the path, you can look into the windows and directly through the house to the setting sun and far below, to the Pacific Ocean.

It's a straightforward house, modest by most standards, but I know it was designed with a lot of thought, because I'm the architect, and the client is my mother.

After living and working as a professor in Fairbanks for nearly 30 years, Mom wanted to escape Alaska's cold, dark winters. She found the perfect site two hours from Portland, in a small beach community called Neskowin.

She wanted a small house (it is 1,500 sq. ft.), that included an office, a quilting room, and a garden that was an integral part of the living space. I knew the local cottage style would be my inspiration and that I'd have to pack a lot into this small house. So I took my design cues from homes in the region, and I used the following five strategies to make the house feel bigger than it really is.

Design multi-use spaces whenever possible

If they're planned with ingenuity, rooms can serve several functions without compromises. The heart of the house is the central common space. This 12-ft. by 20-ft. room with a 17-ft.-tall vaulted ceiling functions as both the living room and the dining room. It's visually linked to the exterior with glass doors and windows that go down to the floor. I didn't have

DINING OUT. Leslie Gordon's house was designed for single living, but it adapts easily to company, thanks to a deck that invites outdoor living. Her son, Tim, was the architect.

TURN UP THE VOLUME. A vaulted ceiling and a wall of glass combine to create the illusion that the living room, located in the center of the house, is twice its size.

WEATHER PERMITTING. The house is sited to take full advantage of ocean views and to protect the homeowner's four-season gardens from offshore winds.

A ROOM FOR QUILTING. (below left) A serious quilter, Leslie needed a dedicated room to work in and a place to store her fabric palette. Custom cubicles in her studio make it easy for her to see her collection, and a sliding quilt wall allows her to pin up her designs as she sews.

A PLACE FOR LAUNDRY, AND GUESTS TOO. The room was designed primarily as a quilting studio, but much of the time it does double-duty as a laundry room. When need be, the appliances are hidden, the quilt wall slides over to act as a screen, the cantilevered table is tucked away, the sofa bed is made up, and the room is transformed into a comfortable guest suite.

a lot of space to work with, so I separated the dining and living areas with subtle changes in flooring and lighting. The dining area floor is at the same level as the entry and kitchen on the other side of the fireplace. The living room area, however, is a step down, and the flooring changes from tile to wood (see the floor plan on p. 91). I emphasized the separation by placing each area on a separately controlled bank of lights.

We also combined the home office and master bedroom into one room. The office has its own distinct corner, with a built-in desk located to take advantage of the view (see the photo above). Facing away from the rest of the room, with its own bank of ceiling lights and surrounded by shelving, the office area feels like a separate space.

We were still left needing a guest room, a quilting studio, space for mechanicals, and a laundry room. We managed to fit them all into one 13-ft. by 14-ft. pavilion on the other side of the entry.

First we had to make sure the room functioned well as a quilting studio, its best and highest calling. The sewing machine sits on a removable cantilevered table next to a long work counter. Mom's fabric palette is in built-in cubicles on the wall. In front, a quilt-design wall rolls back and forth on a stainless-steel rail. The rolling wall usually sits in front of the door to a small mechanical room and moves out of the way when access is needed. The washer and dryer are tucked beneath the work counter, which makes a good surface for folding clothes. When guests stay over, the sewing machine is put away,

cabinet doors block the view of the washer and dryer, and a sofa pulls out to become a bed, transforming the room into a private, comfortable guest suite with its own bath.

Create a space for welcome and transition

An entry, however small, makes a home feel welcoming and eases the transition from the outside. With such a small house, I was not able to devote much room to the entry, so I designed it as a glass breezeway between the quilting studio and the rest of the house and added covered porches on both sides to expand the space. Another trick I used to save space was designing the entry to open to the front garden terrace on one side and the back deck on the other.

Because of the wet Oregon weather and our proximity to the beach, the entry had to be a true mudroom, so we gave the entry storage closet plenty of room for coats, shoes, pet supplies, hiking boots, and backpacks. I also strategically placed the outdoor shower near the deck-side door, with the laundry area in the quilting studio nearby.

A CLEAR PATH. (above and top) Because the entry is tucked between the main house and the quilting studio, the way in had to be crystal clear. The entrance through the garden is flanked by stone columns capped with lights.

A ROOF WITH A VIEW. (above) A distinct outdoor dining room is created by covering just part of the broad deck. It's a natural place for entertaining.

DIVERSITY IN THE GARDEN. (far left) Low walls, decks, concrete benches, and strategically placed plantings all delineate spaces within the sheltered garden.

LIGHT AT THE END OF THE GALLEY. (left) The narrow kitchen has a wide ocean view at the end, making the room feel more spacious.

Extend the living room with gardens and decks

Outdoor rooms increase a home's living space and open up the interior. Besides quilting, Mom's other passion is gardening. She wanted a small, sheltered garden that she could tend 12 months of the year and see from inside the house (see the sidebar on the facing page). So when we designed the garden we thought of it as a series of framed views from the house. Because you can see so much of the landscape from the house, small interior spaces expand as the lush colors and life of the garden are drawn in. In effect, the garden gives our eyes and minds more room to roam.

I think of a deck as an outdoor room, and an extra room of any kind is important in a small house. This deck is large—more than 1,000 sq. ft.—with all of the rooms on the west side opening on to it. But even a small deck gives you another place to go. I designed a covered area just outside the kitchen for dining and entertaining.

MY GARDEN REMINDS ME I'M HOME AT LAST

I RECENTLY READ a research article about how gardening is good for the soul, and I believe it. The Fairbanks, Alaska, growing season is short but strong, and our front yard used to overflow with annuals, perennials, and vegetables. But for 30 years I reluctantly left my garden at the beginning of September after the first hard frost. With little snowfall for protection and cold snaps down to –50°F, even the hardiest perennials often do not survive, and the garden process must begin from scratch every spring.

By contrast, in Neskowin the garden is part of my every day. I can sit in my quilting studio 12 months a year and watch flowers bloom and hear my fountain gurgle. Even better, I can get out into my garden because it is sheltered from the elements by the wrap-around design of the house and garage and the giant Sitka spruce trees. I often spend entire days pruning, repositioning, and adding to the plantings. All of this with the knowledge that I am molding the garden over time and that what I leave in the fall will still be there in the spring. I feel that I have finally found the place I was meant to be.

—Leslie Gordon, homeowner

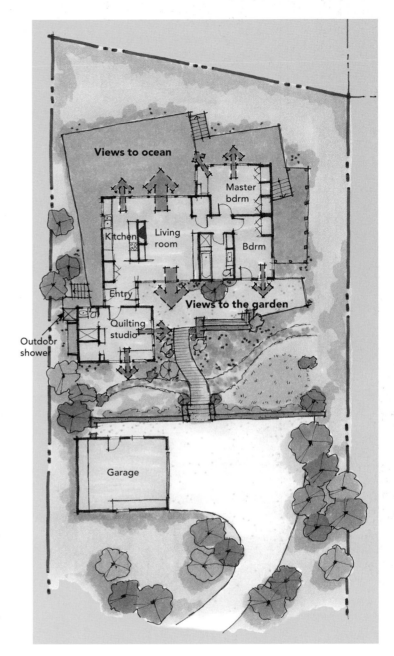

DRAWING THE EYE OUTSIDE

The Gordon home is built on a narrow slice of a lot, with nearby neighbors, woods on three sides, and a spectacular view of the Pacific Ocean. The small house feels more expansive because its windows are strategically placed to take advantage of the ocean and garden views (indicated by the arrows) while keeping neighboring houses out of sight. The decks and many outdoor sitting areas visually extend the sense of space and provide "rooms" for activities beyond the house itself.

SHELF LIFE. (right) So the space
under the hearth wouldn't go to
waste, a narrow wood-storage
bin was built into a shelf there.

Simplify spaces and add storage with built-ins

The more storage and function you build into the structure, the more room you have left to live in. In just about every room we relied on built-in cabinets and shelves for storage and display. You might think that fixtures built into walls would make spaces feel smaller, but the opposite is true. Built-ins allow the lines of the room to remain clean, and they cut down on the amount of furniture that takes up floor space.

The display wall in the living room is a prime example (see the photo at left). We could never duplicate with furniture the amount of storage and display space this built-in affords us. We hid the TV in another built-in above the hearth. And below the hearth is a shelf to hold firewood. This means that the only furniture needed in the living room is a chair, sofa, and side tables.

Recessed lighting also kept the areas uncluttered. Instead of lights suspended from the ceiling or lamps on tables or on the floor, I used directional recessed lights as both task and ambient lighting.

BUILT-INS GIVE YOU ROOM TO MOVE.
Thoughtfully designed display shelves in the
living room and the second bedroom eliminate
the need for additional furnishings, so the
spaces feel more open and roomy.

Use similar materials to connect rooms

One way to make a small house feel larger is to unify spaces with a consistent use of materials, colors, and detailing. I knew the house needed a personality or character that could be repeated throughout, because if you make each space in a small house different, the house will feel even smaller. I created a palette for the trim, tile, flooring, walls, and countertops that I could carry throughout. We trimmed around the doors, windows, and base of the wall with cherry and also used it for a number of the built-ins. To save money, we used cherry-looking melamine for the shelves in the quilting studio. We used hardwood veneer flooring in the living room, the hallway, and the quilting studio.

Throughout the house, wherever we put tile it was uniformly applied. It's all porcelain stone, but the horizontal, or floor, tiles are one color, whereas the tiles on vertical surfaces, such as surrounding the fireplace in the living room, are another. Tying it all together is white linen paint, which makes the house feel light and airy.

Glass is another detail used throughout the house. Glass doors and windows that go down to the floor not only extend the interior space, but also connect rooms by framing the spectacular views.

You can do more, experiment, and take chances with a larger house, but I think that by using fewer materials in a variety of ways I was inspired to do some creative thinking. Looking back, that is one of the things I enjoyed most about the project.

Designing this house was an unbelievable learning experience for me. It allowed me to test some smart, space-saving strategies and stretch my imagination. I feel very lucky that I will be able to see how it ages—gracefully, I hope—over time.

North →

0 2 4 8 ft.

Scale in feet

FEW MATERIALS, USED WISELY

Porcelain stone tile was used in the entry, kitchen, dining area, and baths, wherever the floors were likely to see traffic—and spills.

Both bedrooms were carpeted for warmth and comfort. Although private, they are still a part of the house, so a ribbon of tile was added to the outer edges of the rooms.

Hardwood was used in the living room, hallway, and quilting studio. Note how floors do the work of walls: Tile and hardwood suggest transitions between the living room and the rest of the common rooms.

Because it's so versatile, clean, and durable, simple laminate was selected for counters in the kitchen, bath, and quilting studio.

Cherry built-ins give the home a warm, rich feel, but they can run up a budget, so the cubicles in the quilting studio were made of cherry-looking melamine instead.

Timeless
Character

BY SARAH SUSANKA

I instantly fell in love with this unassuming little cottage designed by John Cole Architect and built by Nathan R. Powell Inc. It has a simple elegance and charm that is much harder to achieve than you might think. Beams, columns, white walls, and natural wood floors and ceilings express the structure without apology or embellishment. The super-simple brackets at each of the alcoves designate these alcoves as separate places while keeping them connected with the larger rooms they participate in.

Christopher Alexander published a book called *The Linz Café* in 1981, just a few years after his paradigm-changing book *A Pattern Language*. A photo at the beginning of that book reminds me of the shot of the lovely office alcove. Indeed, the whole house exemplifies what *A Pattern Language* is all about: It has an effortless sense of place and a timeless character that will endear itself to its inhabitants for a long time. Although it was planned as a guesthouse and is only one phase of a larger project, I'm willing to bet that the owners have bonded deeply with this delightful cottage.

COMFORTABLY SMALL. The open floor plan of the cottage makes it feel much larger than its 900 sq. ft. The long interior views that extend through the oversized windows to the Menduncook River also contribute to the airy and open feeling.

NOOKS AND CRANNIES. (above) Office and window-seat alcoves feel like separate areas yet barely take up any precious floor space.

A Cottage Fit for a Hobbit

BY DEBRA JUDGE SILBER

Asked to design a fitting repository for a client's valuable collection of J.R.R. Tolkien manuscripts and artifacts, architect Peter Archer went to the source—the fantasy novels that describe the abodes of the diminutive Hobbits.

"I came back to my client and said, 'I'm not going to make this look like Hollywood,'" Archer recalled, choosing to focus instead on a finely crafted structure embodying a sense of history and tradition.

The site was critical too—and Archer found the perfect one a short walk away from his client's main house, where an 18th-century dry-laid wall ran through the property. "I thought, wouldn't it be wonderful to build the structure into the wall?"

Not only did the wall anchor the cottage, but stones from another section were used in the cottage's construction. "It literally grew out of the site," Archer said.

Perhaps stranger things have happened in Tolkien's world, but few houses in this one go to such lengths to capture a fictional fantasy in the context of architecture.

CRAFTSMANSHIP AT WORK. David Thorngate of Premium Grade Cabinetry Inc. fabricated the window in his Newark, Delaware, workshop. Made from Spanish cedar, the window measures approximately 98 in. wide by 78 in. tall. Thorngate used more than 30 templates to maintain symmetry for every aspect of the window, completing assembly on top of a full-size template of the window's rough opening

INSPIRED BY LITERATURE AND BY ITS SITE. Archer & Buchanan Architecture Ltd. of Chester County, Pennsylvania, designed this 500-sq.-ft. cottage to house a collection of J.R.R. Tolkien artifacts for an avid collector. Built by Richard Owens of Chester County, the stone and timber-frame structure was inspired by Tolkien's writings.

THE HINGE IS THE TRICK. The round door is hung on a single hinge designed by blacksmith Michael Coldren of North East, Maryland. Designing hardware strong enough to handle the torque of the circular door was one of the tougher challenges, according to the architect. The walls are plywood, trimmed out with Douglas fir details and in-filled with plaster. Above the plaster walls, the roof is supported with Douglas fir rafters and a Glulam® ridge beam, also trimmed with Douglas fir.

A DOOR FIT FOR A HOBBIT. Though the round door is used as an entryway, a more conventionally shaped (and discreetly concealed) 3-ft. by 7-ft. door in the back of the cottage conforms to code and, Archer concedes, makes it easier to get in and out. To the right of the round door, an electrical outlet is disguised under a metal box.

A READING NOOK. Half-walls and an arch create a library in the rear of the main room.

Small-House Secrets

BY CHARLES MILLER

I n "The Purloined Letter," Edgar Allan Poe's mischievous observation on human nature, a stolen correspondence with compromising information is hidden in plain sight. After elaborate investigations have failed to find the letter, Poe's detective spots it pinned to the wall, where no one has bothered to look.

Cathy Schwabe's cottage reminds me of this classic tale. The small house deftly combines a catalog of design strategies that work together to make it feel expansive without ever feeling "designy." These strategies are all right there in plain sight. Seasoned architects and designers know these guidelines, but judging from the fumbled opportunities that plague a lot of small houses being built today, I think they're worth revisiting.

Like the notes in a song, these design strategies do not exist in a vacuum. They are the building blocks of smart small-house design, meant to work together with the goal of creating beautiful, comfortable spaces that fulfill their functions and delight their occupants. They turn up everywhere on a walk through Cathy Schwabe's house tucked amid the redwoods of the California coast.

Raise the ceilings

In the living space, the sloping shed roof rises to
14 ft., where clerestory windows admit north light
and provide ventilation when needed. Notice how
the light from the clerestories bounces off the
white, gypsum-board ceiling, evenly illuminating
the room.

Each of the other rooms has either a cathedral or a
sloping ceiling instead of the standard 8-ft. flat ceiling. If you can't slope a ceiling, raising it to 9 ft. also
will give a small room a surprising lift.

Use scale to your advantage

Exaggerated architectural elements such as the 8-ft.-
tall sliding doors and the three tall double-hung
windows in the west wall speak to generosity. It's
hard to imagine this room with smaller windows
and doors. The vertical shapes of the frames and
glazing echo the vertical lines of the trees in the
background. The black window frames recede, emphasizing the view. Try to imagine them in typical
white. It doesn't work.

BUILT SMALL, FEELS LARGE. In the main living area the oversized windows and patio doors, the raised ceiling, and the extended views all contribute to the large feeling of the room.

DON'T GO OVERBOARD. (below) Using subtle finishes for the cabinets and ceiling allows the texture of the vertical-grain paneling to stand out and make an impact.

Borrow views

The shed roof rises to the north rather than to the south for two good reasons. First, a tall south-facing wall would have added too much solar gain to the room, and more important, there is a forested watershed to the north that will remain forest. The tall windows to the north and west take advantage of these views, and in fact they reinforce the vertical lines of the trees. You can see the treetops through the clerestories.

MAPLE CABINETS

SLATE FLOOR

AVONITE VANITY TOP

LIMESTONE COUNTER

Use texture and color sparingly

The vertical-grain Douglas-fir paneling adds a soothing amber glow and vertical lines of sap and heartwood that reinforce the lines of the windows and tree trunks. The crisp edges where the paneling meets the gypsum-board ceiling emphasize the architecture. Putting fir paneling on the ceiling would have diminished the impact. The ipé floors and maple cabinets have calm grain patterns that don't compete with the fir. The vermilion front door, dining table, and bookcase in the main room add an unmistakable personal touch without going over the top.

Spend money on high-quality materials where it counts

If you're building a small house, you've already saved some money on materials. Invest some of those saved dollars in high-quality hardware, windows, doors, and elegant details. In this house, the fir paneling, ipé flooring, custom solid-wood maple cabinetry, and slate floors in the bath and entry are premium finishes that express the care and thoughtfulness of the designer and builder. Focus on the parts of the house that get plenty of attention and use. The limestone kitchen counter, dotted with fossils, and its undermount stainless-steel sink with integral drainboard are good examples of this. Outside on the patio, the herringbone weave of the cedar bench boards where they turn the corner says that somebody cared. There's just no substitute.

Minimize hallways and make them do double duty

A small house is no place to spend precious space on long, narrow hallways. Instead, centrally locate the entry hall so that rooms can pinwheel around it. This applies to upstairs landings, too. Schwabe allocates a bit of entry space for a bench, which serves as a mini-mudroom for shoes below and a coatrack above. The vermilion door and bright blue bench add a zesty note.

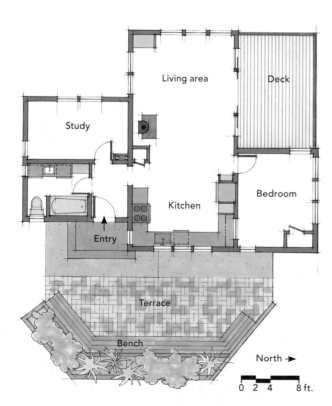

Living area

Deck

Study

Kitchen

Bedroom

Entry

Terrace

Bench

North →

0 2 4   8 ft.

The entry leads either to the bath, the study, or the living space to the north, where the circulation paths to the primary bedroom and the deck merge with the living space, becoming comfortable spatial boundaries between the sitting area and the kitchen/dining area.

Create long interior views

The diagonal views across the living space are only part of what makes the house feel spacious. The view from the entry through the windows in the study is another, as is the sightline from the bath right through the window of the bedroom.

Make multipurpose rooms

The one and only bath is also the laundry room, with a full-size front-loading washer and dryer tucked under the lavatory counter. This strategy not only saves space, but it also minimizes plumbing runs. Likewise, the study is also the guest bedroom.

EXTENDED LIGHTS AND VIEWS. Placing transom windows over interior doors channels daylight and views deep into small spaces.

TWO-IN-ONE. The bathroom and laundry room both occupy the same space, a smart way to save on plumbing and square footage.

BRING THE OUTDOORS IN. The homeowner has brought sunlight in and extended the views by including windows on all four walls of this room.

Use windows on as many sides as possible

We humans like daylight, and when the sun is out we gravitate toward day-lit rooms. To satisfy that need, try to put windows on at least two sides of a room. The great room in this house has windows in all four walls, and a generous skylight over the passageway from the entry hall is a silent guide that says, "Walk this way."

Create private outdoor spaces

Nothing amplifies the perceived size of a small house more than a sunny outdoor space. Here, the sloping lot required a cut in the grade to create a level pad on the uphill side for the entry. Schwabe saw this as an opportunity to carve out a wider pad for a brick terrace. The retaining wall rises about 5 ft. at its highest point. A lower retaining wall in front of it creates a planter between the two for landscaping that screens the neighboring house. Brackets support a yellow-cedar bench.

Just about the time that the sun passes over the patio, it starts to light up the deck off the living space. Tucked into the notch between the bedroom and the living area, the deck becomes a private outdoor retreat.

BRING THE INDOORS OUT. Both the deck off the living area and the terrace off the front of the house extend the living area out of doors.

SPECS

Bedrooms: 1, plus a study that doubles as a guest room
Bathrooms: 1
Size: 800 sq. ft.
Cost: $335 per sq. ft.
Completed: 2006
Location: Gualala, California
Architect: Cathy Schwabe
Builder: Chuck Arana, Marine View Construction

Big River, Small House

BY RUSSELL HAMLET

On a typical morning the closest traffic passing by Michael and Charlotte Green's house is a brood of ducks paddling toward Ross Island to forage. Michael and Charlotte live on the Willamette River—literally.

After raising a family on Bainbridge Island, Washington, the Greens decided to try something completely different. Following their discovery of a tightly knit little community of houseboaters on the outskirts of Portland, Oregon, they concluded that life on the water promised a closer connection to the natural world, freshwater breezes, and constantly changing daylight bouncing off the water.

Their part of the community's dock includes anchorage for two vessels, one on each side of the dock. The main house, which will be about 2,150 sq. ft., will occupy the channel-side mooring. The guest-house shown here is tied up on the riverbank side.

The houseboat marina is in a part of town that has industrial buildings and warehouses scattered along the shore. We followed that lead with finishes that range from simple to rustic. Painted cedar siding, aluminum windows, and a galvanized-metal roof echo the local decor. Inside, birch-plywood built-ins, a galvanized-steel kitchen counter, and rough-sawn fir floors continue this straightforward tone. In a

nod to the rippling surface of the river, corrugated-steel panels play across the ceiling.

The Greens and I had to work with the marina's stringent guest-house rules, which restrict the size of the float that supports the house to no more than 18 ft. by 34 ft., with a maximum height of 15 ft. 6 in. above the water line. The fire department requires access on all sides of a structure, and with the inclusion of an exterior deck, we had a scant 14 ft. 9 in. by 22 ft. 6 in. for the home's footprint. That's not much room for a house with a kitchen, a bathroom, a dining area, a sitting space, and a sleeping loft.

Still, I really enjoy the challenge of designing a house that packs a lot of function and style into a minimum amount of space. This house utilizes nine strategies that can inject maximum utility and character into a small house. You can find multiple examples in each of the photos shown here.

1. Include an outdoor room

Bordered by the house and the kayak rack, this little deck (see the photo on the facing page) has definite boundaries that give it a roomlike sense of enclosure. It simultaneously adds living space and extends the views from inside.

SPECS

Bedrooms: 1
Bathrooms: 1
Size: 433 sq. ft.
Cost: $320 per sq. ft.
(doesn't include float)
Completed: 2008
Location: Portland, Oregon
Architect: Russell Hamlet
Builder: Even Construction

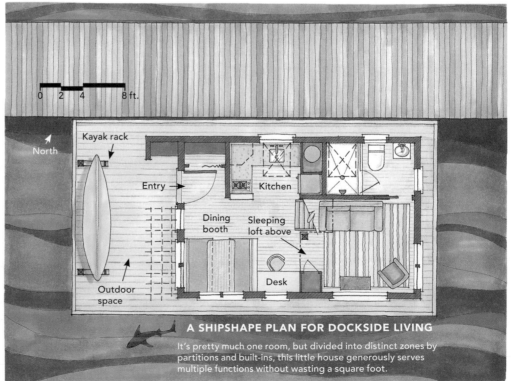

North

Kayak rack

Entry

Kitchen

Dining booth

Sleeping loft above

Desk

Outdoor space

0 2 4 8 ft.

A SHIPSHAPE PLAN FOR DOCKSIDE LIVING

It's pretty much one room, but divided into distinct zones by partitions and built-ins, this little house generously serves multiple functions without wasting a square foot.

EXTEND THE SPACE. Lots of natural light, expansive views, and vaulted ceilings combine to create a space that feels much larger than its 433 sq. ft.

2. Organize the house into zones

Drawing distinctions between different parts of the house based on their function will create the impression of multiple rooms. You can do this with built-ins, ceiling-height and floor-level changes, or different finishes. Although no doors separate them, this house has distinct zones for entry transition, kitchen, dining area, living space, office, and sleeping loft.

3. Include multi-purpose rooms

The living-area couch pulls out to double as a guest bed.

4. Create long views in all directions

We used windows on at least two sides of each zone to provide views and daylight. This variety invites unconfined eye-wandering to stretch the space.

5. Use contrasts in light and color

Light colors on walls and ceilings give a room an open feeling, and sources of daylight at the end of a room draw the eye, expanding the sense of space. During the day the corrugated-metal ceiling constantly changes with the angle of the sun. At night spotlights play across the rippling surfaces, emphasizing the high ceiling.

6. Make the space feel tall

High windows, skylights, the vaulted ceiling, and the open ship's ladder all promote long views to the skyline.

7. Use thick edges and built-ins

Thick edges, such as the partition wall in the loft, give the impression of strength and durability—a good trait in any house. Built-ins, such as the dining booth and the red storage cabinet, always make the most of their space, and they can serve as boundaries that define specific zones.

OPEN IT UP. Skylights allow daylight in and can keep a small space from feeling crowded.

SMART BUILT-INS. The booth provides a built-in dining area and also helps to define the space.

8. Make some things big

The oversize window in the living room evokes a sense of grandeur. In the bath, the 3-ft. by 5-ft. skylit shower (see the photo below) isn't huge, but it's far more generous than the typical elbow-squeezed stalls often found in tiny houses.

9. Invest space in transitions

The sheltered outdoor closet and tiny vestibule just inside the door impart a sense of passage from outside to indoors. It's a subtle but important element that implies a larger structure. The 6-ft.-tall partition between the door and the galley kitchen is both display space and storage on the kitchen side.

A FOUNDATION THAT FLOATS

AT A TIME WHEN IT LOOKED like the surrounding forests were infinite, Oregonians built their houseboats atop raftlike floats made of choice logs. Times have changed. Today, there are two good reasons to take a different approach to building a float for a houseboat: Good logs are getting harder to find, and the logs will eventually need replacing as they rot along the waterline.

The state-of-the-art float supporting the Greens' guesthouse is made of 4-ft.-thick expanded-polystyrene blocks encased in an 8-in.-thick shell of reinforced concrete. Unlike log floats, concrete floats are engineered specifically for the structure they will carry. And unlike log floats, they require little to no maintenance and should last at least 80 to 100 years.

Channels carved into the foam blocks accommodate plumbing and electrical lines and exit the shell at hookup locations on the sides of the float. The topping slab includes a 6-in.-wide stemwall with anchor bolts for tying the building's walls to the float. Point loads such as columns bear on concrete piers that go in holes hogged out of the foam where necessary.

Smaller floats like this one often have "ballast tanks" for adjusting the height of the float. These are basically air pockets that are constructed under the float. The guest-house float has four ballast tanks, one at each corner. Adding some pressurized air to a ballast tank lifts the corner; releasing the air drops it back down.

This float measures 34 ft. by 18 ft., and cost $43,000. At $70 per sq. ft., that's an expensive foundation. But it responds to a demand rarely made of other foundations: Be strong, stable, and lighter than water.

SPACIOUS SHOWER. The shower is larger than you would normally find in a small house, making for a more luxurious feeling bathroom.

DON'T FORGET THE TRANSITIONS. (facing page) The tall partition wall not only provides much needed kitchen storage space; it also creates a transition space at the entry.

Passive House Perfection

BY JUSTIN PAULY

After both growing up in California, Mica and Laureen lived together in many other places throughout their busy careers. Their hearts have always been on the West Coast, though, and they longed to return one day. They eventually found a small piece of property in the coastal enclave of Carmel-by-the Sea on the Monterey Peninsula, and they hired me as architect and Rob Nicely of Carmel Building & Design as builder for a new house that will one day be their permanent home. The collaboration yielded a new type of house for this area, one that appropriately breaks free of the local vernacular while also meeting the country's most aggressive performance benchmarks.

This Passive House is a first for Rob, for me, and for the city of Carmel. Working on this project has confirmed for Rob and me the importance of sustainable, high-performance design and building. For the city and for those who now get to experience this home, I hope the house evokes a realization that design and performance can be held to the same very high standard and that beautiful, exceptionally low-energy homes are within our collective reach.

A fear of passive house

One of the initial challenges with our project was providing Mica and Laureen with the house that they wanted while also convincing Carmel's strict planning commission that the project would complement the existing city fabric. When we first sent the project to the commission, we were so excited about the idea of building Carmel's first Passive House that we included a Passive House brochure. Unfortunately, that decision had the opposite effect of what we hoped. Instead of getting people excited about our project, it scared them into thinking that we were going to build a box with a wall of south-facing glass and few other openings. Although this design might be true of some Passive Houses, our plans called for a different home. Mica and Laureen wanted a contemporary farmhouse with a clean, crisp, and inviting exterior and an interior with an open floor plan that would use a series of outdoor spaces to create a strong relationship with the small yet dramatic site. Fortunately, the commission was able to see that vision, and our plans were approved.

Working around the redwoods

The lot is a 4,000-sq.-ft. flag-shaped parcel hemmed in on three sides by existing homes and on the fourth side by a cluster of massive redwood trees. These redwoods are the dominant feature on the property and became the inspiration for many of the house's design decisions.

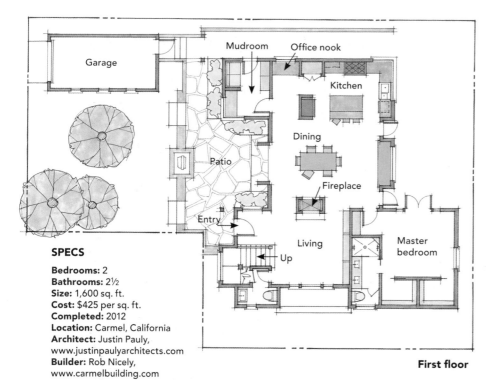

Garage

Mudroom

Office nook

Kitchen

Dining

Patio

Fireplace

Entry

Living

Up

Master bedroom

SPECS

Bedrooms: 2
Bathrooms: 2½
Size: 1,600 sq. ft.
Cost: $425 per sq. ft.
Completed: 2012
Location: Carmel, California
Architect: Justin Pauly,
www.justinpaulyarchitects.com
Builder: Rob Nicely,
www.carmelbuilding.com

First floor

EVOKING COMFORT IN AN OPEN PLAN

The floor plan has carefully designed spaces for gathering and retreat. The core of the plan is the vaulted dining room, which brings people together in the heart of the home. More intimate spaces branch off this central space, and are enriched with elements that make them inviting and comfortable.

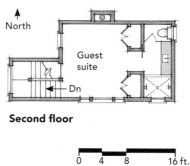

North

Guest suite

Dn

Second floor

0   4   8   16 ft.

CENTER STAGE. With its dramatic vaulted ceiling and massive timbered fan trusses, the dining area occupies the middle of the house. A large bay window floods the space with light from the south, while French doors open the house to the redwoods and patio to the north.

KITCHEN. Light green cabinets topped with polished white macaubas quartzite, not marble, sit in front of a subway-tile backsplash to create a bright, durable space for cooking and entertaining.

The lot's physical and regulatory constraints led us to position most of the house at the rear of the property, with a small single-car garage placed at the street. The garage is linked to the house via a narrow, covered breezeway that steps down slightly to accommodate a subtle change in topography across the site. We placed a small courtyard directly behind the redwood trees and in front of the main living space, and a more private outdoor area directly to the south of the main living space at the rear of the property. The garage and breezeway give the property a "compound" feel, whereas the outdoor areas tie the interior spaces to the exterior site and help to give the compact house a needed sense of openness.

Open spaces and intimate places

In addition to well-connected indoor and outdoor spaces, Mica and Laureen also requested a well-designed kitchen with a large open space nearby for entertaining and smaller, more intimate spaces for relaxing and reading. The compact kitchen and mudroom lie to the north of the dining room; to the south are a small sitting room, a powder room, a master bedroom, and stairs to the second-floor suite. Whereas the vaulted dining room, with large openings to the north and south, lends the house a sense of grandeur, all of the other rooms have a more intimate feel because of their smaller footprint and warm, natural finishes.

A twist on a traditional style

Many of the interior and exterior spaces include traditional elements rendered in more modern detail. Inside, a palette of exposed whitewashed rough-sawn Douglas-fir framing, integral colored plaster, and floorboards made of reclaimed barn wood adds to the warmth of the spaces. Board-and-batten detailing on the upper portion of the fireplace and

HALF-BATH. With a Duravit® sink atop a custom walnut stand set under a Troy® pendant, even the bright, airy half-bath off the living room reinforces elegant farmhouse simplicity.

a large sliding barn door in the upstairs bedroom continue to reinforce the farmhouse aesthetic.

We covered the exterior in white board-and-batten siding that sits atop a continuous water table, with lap siding below to offer a sense of grounding to the home's base. We chose standing-seam zinc-coated metal for the roof, with clear cedar trim for the fascia and underside of the eaves. This boxed-in eave detail gives the whole lid the clean feel of a separate element that has been dropped neatly onto the home below. In addition, the large cedar sliding barn doors and the exaggerated scale of the foursquare window at the stairwell on the north elevation are prominent elements that push the house's style toward the contemporary.

GUEST SUITE. In the small bedroom a sliding barn door with an operable window helps to define the home's farmhouse style and creates privacy at the top of the stairs.

LIVING ROOM. The living room sits beneath a whitewashed Douglas-fir ceiling and before whitewashed Douglas-fir plank walls and custom built-ins. Separated from the grand dining space by only a double-sided fireplace, the living room is very much connected to the hub of the house, while affording respite from the activity within it.

Slashing energy use

The Passive House approach to building hinges on minimizing the amount of energy consumed in a home by providing extremely high levels of insulation and minimizing air leakage. Unlike other rating systems and certification programs, Passive House tends to focus wholly on energy consumption, which has long been a concern for Rob and me.

Several design strategies helped the house to achieve its performance goals. The compact footprint is a key attribute of a super-low-energy building. Furthermore, we maximized the amount of solar gain in the main living areas of the house through generous amounts of southern glazing. Passive Houses tend to minimize the amount of glazing on their north sides, which typically bleed energy

ROOF

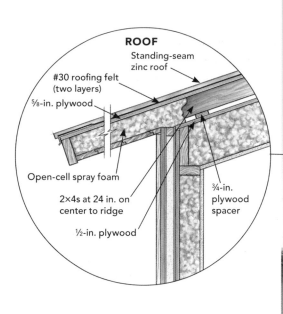

Standing-seam zinc roof

#30 roofing felt (two layers)

⅝-in. plywood

Open-cell spray foam

2×4s at 24 in. on center to ridge

½-in. plywood

¾-in. plywood spacer

FOUNDATION

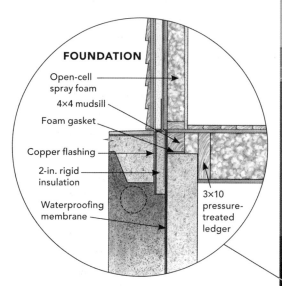

Open-cell spray foam

4×4 mudsill

Foam gasket

Copper flashing

2-in. rigid insulation

Waterproofing membrane

3×10 pressure-treated ledger

COMPONENTS FOR CONSERVATION.
This home consumes as little energy as possible and holds onto that energy for as long as possible through a well-designed envelope. All of the major components have been detailed to ensure optimum performance while being practical to build.

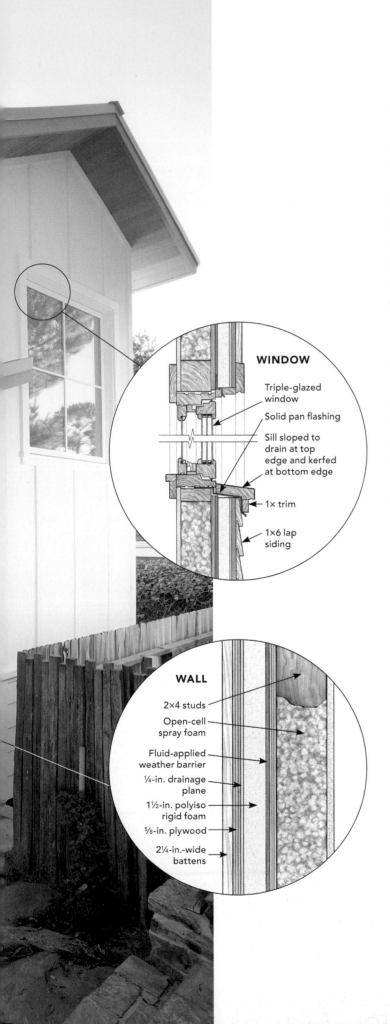

WINDOW

Triple-glazed window

Solid pan flashing

Sill sloped to drain at top edge and kerfed at bottom edge

1× trim

1×6 lap siding

WALL

2×4 studs

Open-cell spray foam

Fluid-applied weather barrier

¼-in. drainage plane

1½-in. polyiso rigid foam

⅝-in. plywood

2¼-in.-wide battens

without providing any positive solar gain. In the case of this house, however, eliminating windows and doors on the north side would have changed the entire look and feel of the house.

Fortunately, we were able to compensate for the large glazed openings to the north by using more insulation in the walls and roof. A combination of advanced-framing techniques and what we consider a "dual-skinned" construction approach to the roof and walls gave us a well-insulated envelope and enabled us to hit our blower-door targets. If the house performs as modeled, it will use approximately 15 percent to 20 percent of the energy consumed by a code-built house.

Our mechanical system is comprised of a Zehnder® heat-recovery ventilator (HRV) that serves two purposes. First, it provides a continuous flow of fresh air into the house. Second, it uses warm indoor air to preheat fresh makeup air through a heat-exchange core to minimize overall heat losses. A hydronic coil added to the HRV serves as a backup heating element. With the obvious exception of certain duct runs, the entire mechanical system lives in a fairly conventional crawlspace under the house. This design detail meant that we had to forgo a concrete slab, which is often used in Passive Houses to store solar energy. As an alternative, we incorporated phase-change materials (PCMs) into the wall assemblies on the south side of the house to serve as a thermal heat sink. PCMs help to regulate indoor temperatures by absorbing excess heat during the day and slowly releasing the heat in the evenings, when the interior temperature dips below the 73°F set point. PCMs simply install as sheets behind the drywall of the interior walls.

Other than the use of PCMs, the construction of this house was intentionally straightforward. I hope that many of the design and construction techniques we used will become mainstream in the years ahead and that high-performance houses such as this will become synonymous with high-end construction.

A Small, Spacious House for a Skinny City Lot

BY
ROXANA VARGAS-GREENAN
AND TRENT GREENAN

As an architect and an urban designer, we like fitting more into a design than there seems to be space for. When we learned the city of Portland, Oregon, was having a design competition for a narrow urban infill house, we jumped at the chance. Portland wanted plans for so-called skinny lots (25 ft. wide by 100 ft. deep) around the city. The impetus for the design competition was to create a narrow house with curb appeal. Our entry could be no wider than 15 ft., yet include a garage.

For livability and marketability, we wanted the design to have at least three bedrooms and large living spaces. It was important for the design elements to reflect the historic architecture of the Portland area. We wanted the interior to be comfortable and uncompromised by the narrowness of the house. Out of more than 400 entries submitted from around the world, our design won a People's Choice Award, and our entry was one of two designs the city chose to offer as permit-ready plans.

Attractive street frontage was the big challenge

At 15 ft. wide, a house has barely enough room for a front door and a garage. We had to include a street-facing garage door because Portland blocks don't have alleys and because the city required the designs

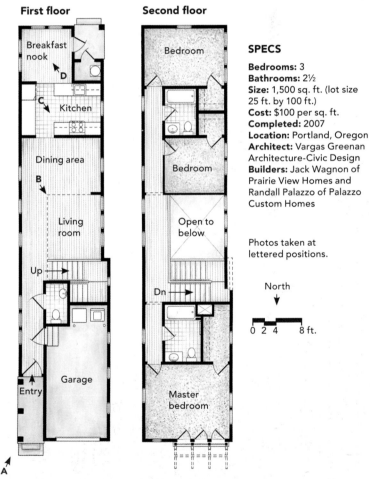

First floor — Breakfast nook, D, C, Kitchen, Dining area, B, Living room, Up, Entry, Garage, A

Second floor — Bedroom, Bedroom, Open to below, Dn, Master bedroom

SPECS

Bedrooms: 3
Bathrooms: 2½
Size: 1,500 sq. ft. (lot size 25 ft. by 100 ft.)
Cost: $100 per sq. ft.
Completed: 2007
Location: Portland, Oregon
Architect: Vargas Greenan Architecture-Civic Design
Builders: Jack Wagnon of Prairie View Homes and Randall Palazzo of Palazzo Custom Homes

Photos taken at lettered positions.

North

0 2 4   8 ft.

APPEAL OF A COMPACT DESIGN

Less square footage benefits the occupants and the builder. Rooms are clustered around high-use areas like the kitchen and the bathrooms. The double height of the living room and its squarish shape provide a central focus. Builder Jack Wagnon likes the centralized plumbing and stacked wall locations for efficiency in building.

LET IN THE LIGHT. The open two-story core of the house serves to connect the different living zones while allowing light to penetrate fully. Photo taken at B on floor plan.

KITCHEN IS CLOSE BUT SEPARATE. The cooking is centralized, but a structural wall blocks the rest of the house from clutter and noise. The breakfast nook at the back of the house is open to the kitchen. Photos taken at D and C on floor plan.

to accommodate parking. A garage, however, is not necessarily the most-attractive element to see from the street.

To reduce the garage's prominence and to create an inviting entry, we added a small porch. This approach offers two advantages. First, it shortens the narrow hallway required to move beyond the depth of the garage when entering the house. It also creates a transitional space for people to pause as they move from the public street to the private home.

We de-emphasized the garage by reducing the size of the door from the standard 8 ft. by 8 ft. to a special-order 7 ft. by 7 ft. In addition, we designed a custom garage door with large windows to help the front of the house feel occupied.

Above the garage, the master-bedroom windows look out to the street. For visual interest, we created a French balcony with cedar 4×4s supporting a shed roof that interrupts the larger roof plane (see the photo p. 120, taken at A on floor plan). These features give the building a welcoming appearance.

We used the narrow footprint to our advantage

It would be easy for a narrow house to feel cramped. However, we wanted to create the opposite effect by emphasizing the strengths of a narrow design. First, in a narrow house, window light easily penetrates to the core. In this design we increased that advantage by creating a two-story living room. Here, the windows extend all the way to the eave. This lets in more sunlight throughout the year, which is a big benefit in the Pacific Northwest, where winters can be cloudy. The height also allows light to penetrate beyond the living spaces into the hallways, which gives the interior a sense of openness.

The vaulted living room also breaks up the linear feel of the house and links different living areas. The master bedroom in front and smaller bedrooms in back are joined by a bridge-like corridor that maintains the bedrooms' privacy but creates a connection to the lower living spaces.

This plan allows for flexibility. The gathering space downstairs can be expanded beyond the living room onto the stairs and into the second-floor hallway as needed during parties. The advantage is that you can incorporate circulation space, which otherwise would be wasted, into active living space. Downstairs, the vaulted room gives the small house a surprising sense of grandeur.

SHEAR-WALL PANELS ALLOW FOR AN OPEN INTERIOR

Providing adequate shear-wall protection is challenging in a long, narrow two-story house with many wall openings. The key to success was using Simpson's® manufactured Strong-Wall® Shearwall panels (www.strongtie.com). Panels are available from 15 in. to 24 in. wide and, depending on the structural needs, are made with either wood or metal webbing that provides shear support. A total of six Strong-Wall panels were used in this house.

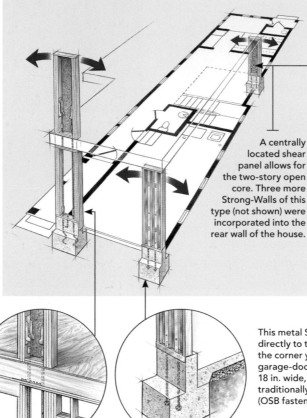

A centrally located shear panel allows for the two-story open core. Three more Strong-Walls of this type (not shown) were incorporated into the rear wall of the house.

Connected to the foundation with 1-in.-dia. steel rods, a second-floor Strong-Wall secures the structure against the seismic and wind-shear loads that a tall, skinny building might encounter.

This metal Strong-Wall is bolted directly to the footing. It secures the corner yet leaves room for the garage-door opening. At only 18 in. wide, it replaces a 4-ft.-wide traditionally framed shear wall (OSB fastened to studs).

Affordability Is a balancing act

We want our designs to be affordable, but stripping a house to its basics would not help the city to establish attractive urban infill. To retain important details, we prioritized design elements. Outside, the most important elements are the recessed windows, the French balcony, and the wooden garage door with windows. In addition, we recommend high-quality environmentally friendly paints and finishes, an open floor plan, and a double-height living room.

To reduce energy costs and to be certified by the local green-building body (www.earthadvantage.org),

we reduced the floor-to-window ratio to less than 25 percent. In addition, we increased the floor joists from 2×8s to 2×10s to get R-38 insulation under the house. In the attic, we achieved R-49 and R-38 in the areas with scissors trusses.

We made some compromises to reduce costs. For example, we re-engineered the foundation to reduce the volume of concrete used. We provided options for fixed instead of operable windows. We also repeated window configurations when possible and found affordable window and door options that matched our design standards.

A Tiny Addition for a Growing Family

BY TINA GOVAN

My husband and I moved into our 1923 bungalow in downtown Raleigh, North Carolina, as a young couple. Ten years, two children, and one dog later, the house had become cramped. Having lived in Japan, we were accustomed to tight quarters, but the constraints of 1,000 sq. ft. had become too great, especially with the added demands of my home office. We chose to add on to our home instead of moving and had a lot of needs to accommodate, but not a lot of space to do it.

For two years, I worked as an architect in Japan and admired how the Japanese were able to introduce a sense of expansiveness within the smallest of structures. It was through my observations there that I developed many of my own design ideas. With a strong reliance on those strategies, I approached the challenge of designing our tiny addition.

Soft spatial boundaries allow multiuse spaces

Using changes in ceiling height, floor level, or materials; using partial or sliding walls rather than solid, full-height ones; using pocket doors rather than swinging doors; and carving niches within larger spaces are all strategies I used for distinguishing spaces in a softer way.

The main common room, or plaza, of the addition needed to serve a wide range of functions. To keep the area open and to avoid separate rooms for each use, I created small but distinctive spaces along the edges of a high central living area.

One corner of the addition provides a dining space surrounded by a bank of windows, whereas the other accommodates my home office. The tatami room (our new bedroom) is raised several steps above the main living area. Tucked into another corner is a stacked washer/dryer unit that is hidden

FREE-FLOWING AND FUNCTIONAL. The addition is not defined by rooms and walls, but by open spaces that serve a variety of tasks. Southern yellow pine adds rich trim details throughout, while a roof comprised of rigid-foam insulation, A/C plywood, and cable collar ties helps to keep the bones of the structure in focus. Photo taken at B. Photo on p. 125 taken at A.

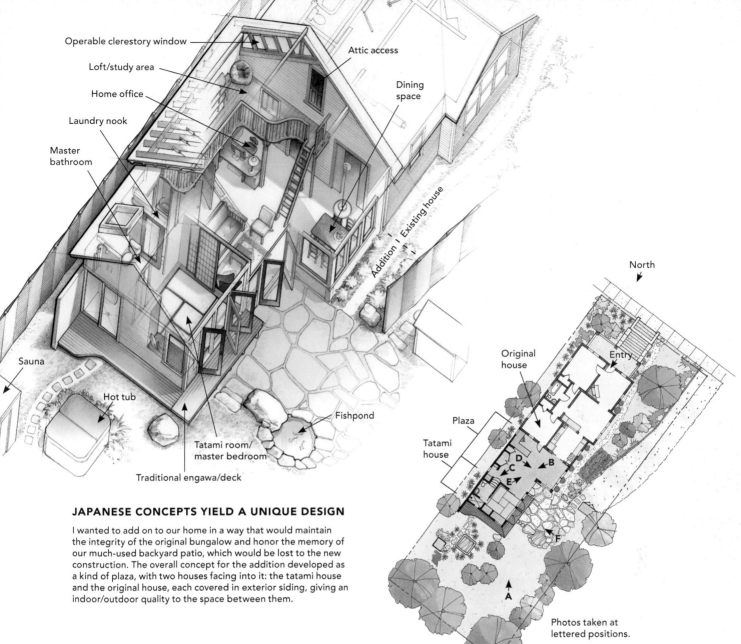

Operable clerestory window

Loft/study area

Home office

Laundry nook

Master bathroom

Attic access

Dining space

Addition | Existing house

Sauna

Hot tub

Fishpond

Tatami room/ master bedroom

Traditional engawa/deck

North

Entry

Original house

Plaza

Tatami house

D
C
B
E
F
A

Photos taken at lettered positions.

0   8   16   32 ft.

JAPANESE CONCEPTS YIELD A UNIQUE DESIGN

I wanted to add on to our home in a way that would maintain the integrity of the original bungalow and honor the memory of our much-used backyard patio, which would be lost to the new construction. The overall concept for the addition developed as a kind of plaza, with two houses facing into it: the tatami house and the original house, each covered in exterior siding, giving an indoor/outdoor quality to the space between them.

behind a sliding plywood panel held in place with a simple wooden peg. A counter and hamper sit opposite. This design allows the laundry area to coexist with more-public spaces and also saves valuable square footage.

Another example of this kind of space is the loft, which wraps two sides of the plaza. It allows us to inhabit the high volume of the room and serves as a private getaway with a small library and its own view of life below.

Softer boundaries also affect the family dynamic. By designing one common space with smaller spaces carved within it, we can be together as a family yet remain comfortably separate, engaged in different activities.

Flexibility and long views make the house work

In a continued effort to keep the house open, I was faced with a huge dilemma: How could I add a private master bedroom and bathroom to the back of the house without blocking views, light, and access to the backyard? I wondered if a space could be both public and private.

Again, drawing from my experience in Japan, I chose to loosen the idea of "bedroom" and treat it as a space that could accommodate private use at night

LIGHT BRINGS THE SPACE TO LIFE. Carefully placed windows draw sunlight deep into the addition, illuminating interior details, shapes, and textures. Wherever light enters the space, an equally valuable view extends out. Photo taken at C on floor plan.

BRING THE OUTDOORS IN. Large windows strengthen the indoor/outdoor connection, while a thin window in the dining space cleverly marks the transition between the old house and the new addition. Photo taken at D on floor plan

and other uses during the day. A traditional tatami room offered the flexibility I wanted. Custom-made shoji screens disappear for openness or slide out for privacy while still allowing light to penetrate. This room makes possible long sightlines, which would otherwise have been cut off by a traditional bedroom. What might have been a solid box is now open, providing a place for sleep, yoga, after-sauna relaxation, or as we have discovered, a stage for our kids. The ability to open this "private" bedroom to other functions, as well as to sunlight, views, and access to the outside, is absolutely essential in making our small house feel spacious.

Similarly, the master bathroom was built along a short hallway leading to the outdoor hot tub and sauna. When needed, the bathroom is transformed into a private area by sliding a frosted-glass door out from behind the toilet. This door does double duty as a cabinet door, covering storage shelves above the toilet when open and allowing access to them when shut.

Hidden storage areas increase space efficiency

Keeping our addition organized is crucial. Typically, opportunities for storage lie under stairs, under roof eaves, above and below window seats, and in other often-overlooked areas. By building thicker walls, you can tuck a bookcase, a linen closet, or a stacked washer/dryer into a hallway or niche.

In our project, I took advantage of as many storage opportunities as possible. By thickening the back wall of the tatami room I could add a built-in window seat and closet to provide storage for our bed, which is a futon, and clothes. This built-in assembly is below a large storage shelf that holds books and CDs. The attic space above the tatami room, which is accessed by a stepladder and sliding panels high in the master bathroom, keeps sweaters, jackets, and other winter items. Also, three large closets sit below the much-used loft, which has given new use and easy access to what once was a nearly inaccessible attic.

Outdoor rooms increase usable square footage

On our tight 50-ft. by 130-ft. city lot, efficient use of outdoor space is important. By placing a patio immediately outside the common room and a wraparound deck (known as an *engawa* in Japan) outside the tatami room, doors can be flung open and interior spaces can spill outdoors. Similarly, the bathroom is continuous with the garden through sliding-glass doors and a concrete wall that extends out.

By building a fence that surrounds the house we were able to define outdoor living "rooms." Paradoxically, this fence makes the yard feel larger rather than smaller and allowed us to create intimate gardens between the house and the property border.

In the same way that fences can create a private oasis in the midst of a dense neighborhood, carefully planned windows can edit out the visual clutter of immediate neighbors and focus attention on selected pieces of the landscape. In this way, as the Japanese practice, you can achieve a sense of space as well as privacy both inside and out, with neighbors just feet away. Density need not feel dense.

BREAKING THE BARRIER BETWEEN INDOOR AND OUTDOOR SPACES. The tatami room's three doors open to the deck and patio, expanding the room's feel. Photo taken at F on floor plan.

CONNECTED BUT SEPARATE. Along with matching French doors, the large windows of the main living space offer a nearly uninterrupted view of the patio, fishpond, and yard. Clerestory windows in each gable cast a blanket of light and provide views of treetops near and far. Photo taken at E on floor plan.

GOOD BONES. The original house (facing page) had plenty of appealing features but an addition was necessary to accommodate all the home-owners were looking for. Photo taken at A on floor plan. Before photo taken at B.

A New Floor Plan Saves an Old House

BY PARKER PLATT

Brevard is a small town nestled in the mountains of western North Carolina. It was developed around a combination of industry and tourism, and today it's a thriving community rich in outdoor recreation and the arts.

Our home is in the Railroad Avenue district, the neighborhood developed around the town's depot, originally home to essential businesses such as a livery, an icehouse, a cotton mill, and a lumber company. The houses built in this area were a mixture of merchants' homes and boardinghouses that served visitors arriving from the depot.

Our Craftsman-style bungalow was built in 1910, and a small boardinghouse was added to the property a few years after that. When we purchased both houses in 2009 they had been abandoned for years. We bought our houses as part of a collection of seven abandoned houses. All have been or are currently being renovated, as the neighborhood has become the focus of public and private revitalization planning and investment.

There is a lot we like about our old houses. They are small and well built. The detailing is simple but strong. As we found them, the houses were shells with great maple floors, 10-ft.-tall ceilings, large windows and doors, and elegant trim and molding details that we've largely kept intact. Overall,

the general layout of the main house was good, but it lacked adequate storage, comfortable bathroom space, a modern kitchen, and the general amenities and functional areas a modern lifestyle demands. The revitalization of this house was an exploration in space planning. We removed, moved, and added walls to carve out better spaces within the old footprint. When our design goals exceeded the capacity of the old structure—as was the case with our desire for a master suite, for instance—we added on.

The changes we made to our home are not necessarily bungalow specific. Many houses share similar attributes, and they need similar design improvements to make them practical, comfortable, and pleasing places to live.

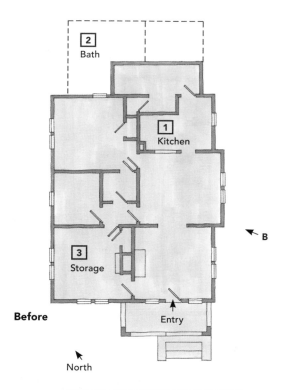

2
Bath

1
Kitchen

B

3
Storage

Before

Entry

North

Pantry

E

Master
bedroom

Kitchen

Laundry

C

Dining
room

D

Bedroom

Living
room

After

0 2 4   8 ft.

Entry

A

BEFORE AND AFTER:
THREE AREAS OF IMPROVEMENT

When redesigning the main house, the author focused on three primary living spaces: the kitchen, the bathrooms, and general storage areas. Nearly all the upgrades could be accommodated in the original footprint, but the house needed an addition to make it really work.

SPECS

Bedrooms: main house, 2; guesthouse, 1
Bathrooms: main house, 2; guesthouse, 1
Size: main house, 1,488 sq. ft.;
guesthouse, 648 sq. ft.
Cost: $150 per sq. ft.
Completed: 2010
Location: Brevard, North Carolina
Architect: Parker Platt
Builder: Anthony Randolph

Photos taken at
lettered positions.

Connect the kitchen

Older houses are often well proportioned with comfortably sized rooms, tall ceilings, and large windows that provide plenty of light and air circulation—important qualities in the days before air-conditioning. However, rooms are often disconnected from each other and don't allow for the open living spaces desirable today.

Kitchens, for example, were isolated rooms with ever-changing storage options and appliances. In 1910 there may or may not have been running water in our kitchen, and it likely had a wood-burning cookstove placed in a corner. The kitchen had been updated over the years. The work wasn't always well done, though, and the space was never fully modernized. With a couple of simple design changes between our kitchen and dining space, we opened the house from the front porch to the kitchen and back door. The spaces—living, dining, and kitchen—are clearly defined, but they remain open and connected. All our public spaces now "live together," our kitchen is functional and comfortable, and our house feels a little bit larger.

OPEN THE KITCHEN AND ADD STORAGE

At some point a pass-through was created in the wall separating the kitchen and the dining room. Now a peninsula separates the two spaces; its raised bar topped with reclaimed oak provides a gathering and serving area. A new pantry between the back door and the kitchen catches groceries as they come in from the car, and a reclaimed-oak desk beside the refrigerator serves as command central for the house.

Pantry increases function and decreases clutter in the kitchen.

This wall was removed to open sightlines through adjacent spaces.

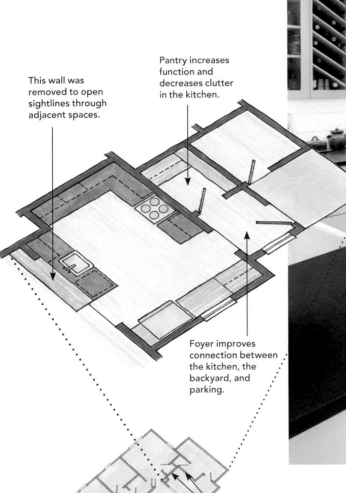

Foyer improves connection between the kitchen, the backyard, and parking.

Walls were removed to increase the size of the kitchen.

OPENED UP AND MODERNIZED. The kitchen was fully modernized and walls were removed to increase its size and open it up to the rest of the house. Photo taken at C on floor plan.

Upgrade the bathrooms

Old houses never have accommodating bathrooms by today's standards. It's not uncommon to find a 50- to 75-year-old, four- to five-bedroom house with a single bathroom; a whole family commonly shared a single bath. Although every house should have at least one tub for bathing kids and for other occasional needs, most of us now prefer to shower.

By fully renovating our existing bath in the simple style of the house, we got a comfortable guest bathroom that has a tub and that is open to the hall. We added a private second bath with a large shower off our bedroom as part of an addition packed full of function.

CREATIVE DAYLIGHTING. The addition that includes the master bath is 26 ft. wide. This will allow the easy addition of a car shelter in the future. For that reason, there are no windows on the back wall. To get daylight into this space, a window was included in the toilet room and over the vanity a skylight was added that floods the center of the bathroom with light. Photo taken at E on floor plan.

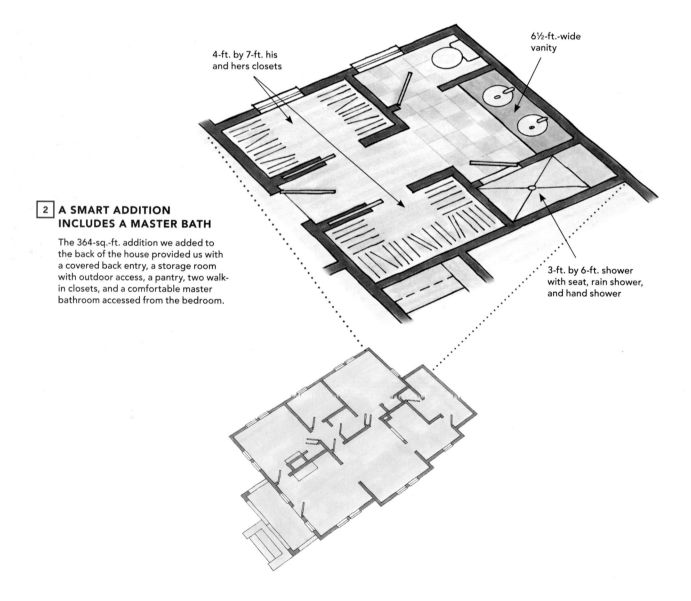

4-ft. by 7-ft. his and hers closets

6½-ft.-wide vanity

3-ft. by 6-ft. shower with seat, rain shower, and hand shower

2 | A SMART ADDITION INCLUDES A MASTER BATH

The 364-sq.-ft. addition we added to the back of the house provided us with a covered back entry, a storage room with outdoor access, a pantry, two walk-in closets, and a comfortable master bathroom accessed from the bedroom.

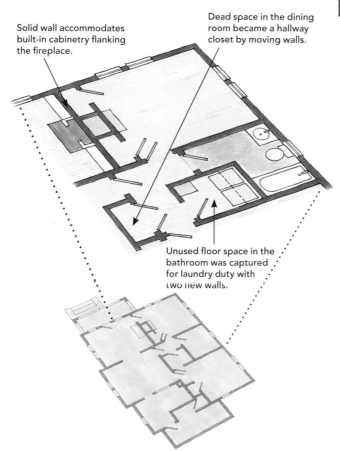

Solid wall accommodates built-in cabinetry flanking the fireplace.

Dead space in the dining room became a hallway closet by moving walls.

Unused floor space in the bathroom was captured for laundry duty with two new walls.

3 **CLOSETS IMPROVE COMFORT**

When it came to improving storage, creative use of existing floor space was critical. The walls between the dining room and bathroom were drastically rearranged to make way for two closets and a laundry room.

Increase storage

Beyond chopped-up floor plans and inadequate bathroom spaces, older houses lack the kind of storage we now find necessary. Somehow people managed to leave their houses well dressed and pressed every day with a fraction of the closet space we now expect. As part of our small addition, we also added an outdoor storage room, a pantry, and two walk-in closets. We made small internal changes to our floor plan as well to add a closet in the guest room and a coat closet in the hall. We also created a laundry space that improved the functionality of the house.

Old houses didn't have the mechanical systems necessary in modern homes, and those mechanical systems need a place to live. Fortunately, we were able to place mechanicals so that they didn't deprive us of valuable floor space. We used a geothermal HVAC system to condition the main house by

BUILT-INS ADD STORAGE. (facing page) Subtle changes were made in the wall between the guest bedroom and the living room to enable the addition of a closet on the private side of the wall and built-in cabinet space on the public side. Photo taken at D on floor plan.

running pipes in trenches in the yard. This system doesn't require an outdoor unit. The indoor unit is in the attic. Our water heater is in a partial basement under our master bedroom.

A home worth preserving

Large numbers of beautiful old houses built from the late 1800s through the 1940s line the streets of central neighborhoods close to the activity of town. Empty lots in such places are hard to come by. Older homes also have elements you don't readily find in new houses: built-up trim details and classic mantels, hardwood floors, and solid old-growth framing.

Homebuilders of old regularly relied on plan and detail books published by architects and designers, and they developed a good sense of proportion and quality.

An old house has stories that can be as interesting as the house itself. At the closing, our attorney told us that he used to spend time in the main house as a child with his friend John Huggins. After we renovated the house, we were invited to speak to the local historical society about our efforts in the neighborhood. John Huggins was in the audience that night and approached us after we spoke. He let us know that he was happy with what we had done with the place. John, now in his late 70s, told us that he was born in our house and that he and his wife spent their wedding night and first year of marriage in the guesthouse now used by my in-laws.

As an architect with a residential focus, I am aware of cost and quality in new construction projects. When we took stock of our renovation, it was clear that for the amount we invested we could not have achieved the location or the quality of home if we had built new. Perhaps just as important, we wouldn't have helped to preserve such a rich local history.

THE MISSING LINK

THE SMALL WHITE HOUSE added to the property around 1915 was close to the back of our main house, which sits where it was originally built on the half-acre lot. The small house's location didn't allow for the addition we had imagined, and it blocked the main house from access to and views of the large backyard. We moved the small structure (see the top photo below) to the rear of the site and converted it to a guesthouse that would perfectly accommodate my wife's parents, who come for extended stays from Switzerland.

The guesthouse was a blank slate when we bought it. Ultimately, we changed it from a two-bedroom house with a small living space to a one-bedroom cottage with a combined kitchen and living area and a large covered front porch.

The cottage makes good use of our entire lot and relieves some of the demand that would otherwise be placed on our small home.

A Better House, Not a Bigger One

BY SIGRID SIMONSON

With the friendly face of a suntanned surfer, our contractor, Tony Hunter, looks approachable. That might explain why so many total strangers felt free to offer their opinions about the one-story house he was building for my husband, Bob Manwaring, and me. "Where is the second story?" and "Are they crazy?" were two common queries Tony fielded on an almost daily basis during the construction phase.

No one can remember the last time a permit was issued for a one-story house in our neighborhood. We live in a small island community in southern California, where the typical lot size is 30 ft. wide by 80 ft. long. With no room to expand laterally, two- and three-story homes are being built to replace the smaller ones that once lined our tiny streets and canals. As a result, some of the funky charm that characterized our neighborhood is being lost.

We moved here several years ago, into a 680-sq.-ft. former rental home not much larger than a double-wide trailer. It not only was small, it felt small. It wasn't long before we—like our neighbors—started planning to replace the house with one better suited to comfortable year-round living.

A TIGHT SHIP. (facing page) A captain's bed, inspired by the reading nooks in Sarah Susanka's book *The Not So Big House*, fit neatly into the homeowners' plan to build a house that didn't waste an inch. Not only does it have the playful appeal of a ship's berth, but it also transforms instantly into a private "guest suite" with its own bath when the pocket doors just beyond the kitchen are closed.

SMALL BUT STANDING TALL. (right) Sigrid and Bob raised the foundation of their new home 27 in. above street level to provide privacy from passers-by and help it stand out beside its two-story neighbors.

SMART MOVES FOR A SMALL HOME

Features that make the most of limited space are designed into every room of Sigrid and Bob's home. But the skylights, built-ins, and pocket doors lend more than a few extra inches: They also introduce enough charm and character to fill a house twice its size.

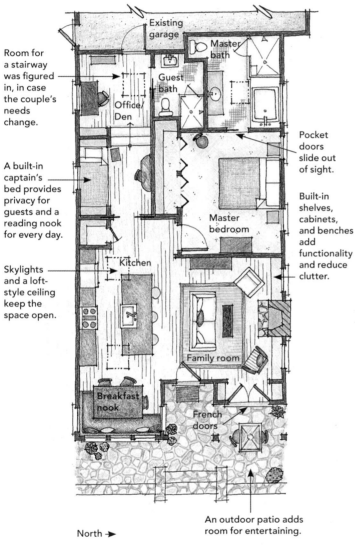

Room for a stairway was figured in, in case the couple's needs change.

A built-in captain's bed provides privacy for guests and a reading nook for every day.

Skylights and a loft-style ceiling keep the space open.

Existing garage

Master bath

Guest bath

Office/ Den

Pocket doors slide out of sight.

Built-in shelves, cabinets, and benches add functionality and reduce clutter.

Master bedroom

Kitchen

Family room

Breakfast nook

French doors

North ➤

0 1 2 4 6 ft.

Scale in fee

An outdoor patio adds room for entertaining.

Bob and I spent many months contemplating what size house to build. We are empty-nest baby boomers with no grandchildren in the foreseeable future. The common wisdom was to build a home with maximum resale value should we wish to move. But did we need all that space? And could we afford the quality workmanship, appliances, and materials we wanted if we built a larger home? The cost of home construction, we knew, follows a simple formula of dollars per square foot. With a specific budget in mind, we calculated the cost of building a home with high-end workmanship, materials, and appliances. The answer was soon obvious: We could build the house we wanted if we kept it small.

Uncertain of what to do, we invited Charles Lane, a local realtor and dear friend, over for a glass of wine and described our dilemma. His advice was simple: Build the house you want to live in.

So as an exercise we made a list of exactly—and only—what we needed to live and entertain:

- One room to "live" in with multiple doors opening to the outside.
- An open kitchen with a big island (which could also be used for things other than food preparation).
- One bedroom large enough to accommodate a king-size bed.
- Two bathrooms, one with a deep tub.
- Well-organized closet space.
- A dining area large enough to seat our long-running dinner group of eight people.
- A small home office with room for a computer and space to pay bills, etc.
- A private place for an overnight guest to sleep and an adjacent bath.
- Lots of outdoor entertaining and living space, with room for pots and planted areas.

After many floor-plan doodles, scribbles, and revisions, we called in architect Jeff Jeannette to discuss our unconventional concept. We wanted to build a casual "beach house" on one level, with high ceilings for a loft-like feel. The resulting structure would

RAISE THE CEILING.
Given the house's small size, the single most dramatic way to create a feeling of spaciousness was to raise the ceiling.

USE POCKET DOORS.
The small size of the house made pocket doors a necessity. In some locations there is simply not enough space for a standard door to swing open. The doors adjacent to the captain's bed, for example, are completely hidden until pulled out, but are key to a flexible floor plan.

measure less than 1,200 sq. ft. We chose Jeff because he came highly recommended, we'd seen his work, and we felt he was willing to collaborate—rather than make a personal statement—on the design of our home. It proved to be a great decision. During our first meeting I presented story boards, like the ones I use for my design work, as a visual aid to help describe our ideas. To this he added his own measure of creativity, knowledge, and experience

and returned with a great plan that required little revision. And he remained involved throughout the building process, always available to answer unanticipated questions.

Intrigued by that concept of loft living, we let that vision guide our choice of which interior walls to extend to the ceiling and which to leave at a header height of 9 ft. An exposed forced-air heater duct and skylights also emphasize the loft feel and draw the

BUILD IT IN. (above left) A house this small requires a lot of built-in storage to control clutter, so every room in the house makes use of deep drawers, cupboards, and shelves. Cupboards along the fireplace wall house stereo and TV equipment. Drawers under the banquette and the captain's bed hold oversize serving items and extra bedding.

CREATE THE ILLUSION OF SPACE. (above right) Kitchen cabinets are designed one foot taller than standard (another visual trick to draw the eye upward), allowing for seldom-used items to be placed above.

eye upward. Occasionally I have tried to visualize what our house would have been like with traditional 8-ft. ceilings. Although the footprint would have been identical, the sensation of a lower ceiling seems almost claustrophobic. It's amazing what psychological space a high ceiling provides.

Building a small house, we discovered, isn't a matter of just shrinking everything down to size. We used specific strategies and design elements, beyond raising ceiling heights, to help our small home seem more spacious (see p. 140 and 144). And as satisfied as we are with the small scale of our new house, we did provide for the possibility of a phase two: an additional two bedrooms and bath over the attached garage at the rear of the house. In this design, our office area would be replaced by a stairway that would ascend to the top of the existing 530-sq.-ft. garage, which was designed with reinforcements to carry the weight of a second story.

Now that our home is complete, we're the ones hearing the comments, and they sound like this: "If we didn't have so much stuff, we could live like you do." Or "The truth is, we live in only three rooms— our bedroom, den, and kitchen. That's exactly what you've built." Or—my husband's favorite— "Congratulations, dude, you've built a purely selfish house."

SPLURGE OR SAVE? (below) Sigrid did both. For the sconces over the captain's bed she selected $130 copies (top) rather than the designer originals. In the bath she used reasonably priced tiles from Walker Zanger's® Soho series to avoid the look of flat "machine-made" tiles (center). But she shelled out for a pricey Dornbracht® faucet (bottom) "for its sculptural beauty and because it can be seen from all angles of the house."

EXPAND SPACE OUTDOORS. (facing page and above) A raised stone patio adds 375 sq. ft. of outdoor living space, easily accessible through the front door as well as from a pair of French doors off the living room. A wrought-iron table and chairs at one end and recycled-wood Adirondack chairs at the other make these two areas the summertime dining and living rooms.

FURNISHING TO FIT

AFTER LIVING IN A HOME with 2,000 sq. ft., here's how Sigrid and Bob fit their furniture and possessions into a much smaller space:

START WITH PLACEMENT

During the framing stage, the couple determined the precise location of their seven major furniture pieces by moving newspaper templates about the floor so that electrical outlets and TV cables could be properly positioned. Sigrid also made rough scale drawings of the sconces she had selected and taped them up at various heights around the rooms to determine their best height relative to the furniture before the wiring was done.

REFRESH WITH SLIPCOVERS

In a small house with few rooms, it's important to be able to change the scenery from time to time. So when Sigrid ordered the sofa she ordered two sets of slipcovers (spring and fall "wardrobes") and had the factory make two for the existing chair as well. This strategy also helps prevent excessive wear.

FILL IN WITH "PART-TIME" FURNITURE

The couple purchased six stackable Bellini chairs from Heller after seeing them at a local cafe. Two are used as dining chairs. The others store compactly in the garage, if needed for additional seating. Small wooden stools and benches are scattered throughout the house, filling in as end tables and stepstools as needed.

DON'T SACRIFICE COMFORT FOR SCALE

Sigrid's philosophy for furnishing smaller spaces is to use a few large pieces rather than multiple small ones. That meant making sure the bedroom was large enough to accommodate a king-size bed and a favorite pine armoire rather than buy a smaller bed and dresser.

SITE SENSITIVE. Placing the house in a small clearing preserves aspects of the site that made it an attractive place to build. Cedar shingles and a metal roof are durable and low maintenance, and complement the setting. Photo taken at A. Photo on the facing page taken at B.

Build Like This

BY MATTHEW O'MALIA

I n 2008, when my business partner and I decided
to form a design/build firm, we agreed to build to
the highest standard of sustainability and to do so
cost-effectively. With all our projects, we hoped to
achieve a synergy between designing for human
comfort, building in response to the site, and achiev-
ing long-term durability. We quickly agreed that the
Passive House standard would be the most compre-
hensive and clear measure of our success. To
demonstrate that we had the ability to reach the
standard, we built our first prototype, a house we
called the GO Home. To reach the Passive House
standard in Maine's cold climate, we developed a
new way to design and build homes collaboratively.
The GO Home, completed in 2009, was Passive
House certified, achieved LEED platinum, and was
named the U.S. Green Building Council's residential
project of the year.

Since building the GO Home we've refined our
design-and-build approach in completing several
other high-performance projects. This house in Bath,
Maine, is based on one of our design-plan packages
that delivers (depending on the site) a house that
could meet the Passive House standard, that's comfortable and attractive, and that has a modest base
cost—roughly $160 per sq. ft. Here is how we achieve
such grand results on such a low budget.

Design it to be compact

Wendy and Bill came to us because they were interested in building the smallest and most sustainable
home they could for their retirement. Of the plans
we offer, they chose to work with our 1,000-sq.-ft.
plan, which includes one bedroom; two bathrooms;
an open kitchen, dining, and living space; and a
small study.

The shape of the house was influenced by our
desire to create a simple but well-proportioned
home. The main living space lies beneath the gabled
portion of the house, with the supporting functions
beneath a shed roof that wraps the side and back of
this main space. The entry porch is recessed under

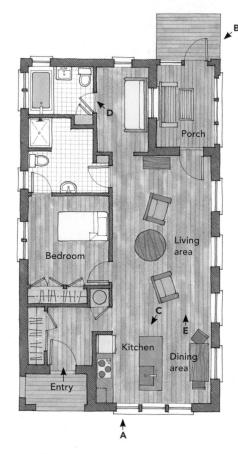

North

Entry

Bedroom

Living
area

Porch

Kitchen

Dining
area

DESIGNED FOR COMFORT AND FLEXIBILITY

The footprint of this house is a simple rectangle. There are no complicated jogs in the exterior walls, which makes insulating and air-sealing easier. The plan is also flexible in the arrangement of spaces. For example, the plan easily can be adapted for a client who needs a two-bedroom home, and the placement of the kitchen, living, and dining areas is adjustable. Beyond the interior, two outdoor spaces influence the living experience. A covered entry, an asset to any house, is especially important in regions that have seasonally inclement weather. A screened-in porch, which is carved into the back corner of the house, creates a retreat that can be used as a getaway for the homeowners—an important feature in a small home—or for entertaining guests.

SPECS

Bedrooms: 1
Bathrooms: 2
Size: 1,000 sq. ft.
Cost: $160 per sq. ft. (base plan)
Completed: 2011
Location: Bath, Maine
Architect: Matthew O'Malia; www.GOLogic.us
Builder: Alan Gibson; www.GOLogic.us
Annual energy expenses: $1,000 (8,124kwh)

Photos taken at
lettered positions.

0   2   4   8 ft.

the shed roof on the south facade, and the screened-in porch is carved into the northeast corner of the house.

To create interior spaces that have a small footprint but still feel generous, we designed an open floor plan for the kitchen, living, and dining areas. These spaces also provide direct access to the bedroom and the bathrooms to avoid hallways and redundant circulation. We also increased the height of the ceiling to 9 ft. and the size of the windows in the main space. The result is an open interior with a strong exterior connection.

Adapt it to its site

Wendy and Bill's site was challenging, and in many ways it tempered the performance potential of the house. The site is surrounded by beautiful, mature hardwood trees, which made it difficult to get the solar gain required for the Passive House standard. We all agreed that the trees were more important than the standard, given that the house would still perform exceptionally well.

The house plan was developed with the intention of having its longest axis running east to west so that the living-room wall full of windows would face the sun to the south. On this narrow site, however, the longest axis runs north to south, and the window-filled living-room wall faces east. Although the siting of the house doesn't provide ideal access to the sun, it does provide terrific views. We didn't totally give up on passive solar gain, though. We modified the plan and placed three massive tilt-turn windows on the south-facing gable end. The windows provide abundant daylight in the kitchen, dining, and living areas and much-needed solar gain during the heating season. Such large windows in a small house also create an unexpected but welcoming look upon approach and give the simple house character.

Make it efficient and buildable

Our version of high-performance, cost-effective construction relies on a superinsulated slab on grade, hybrid SIP walls, a truss roof, triple-glazed German windows, and mechanical ventilation with heat recovery.

A TAILORED FIT. White-oak cabinets topped with soapstone countertops offer just enough storage in the kitchen, which isn't designed for entertaining but for simple meal prep. Door-size windows bring daylight into the space, which sits between a small dining area and the main entry. Photo taken at C on floor plan.

We build atop a slab for several reasons. Most important, a slab-on-grade foundation is the most cost-effective way of providing high levels of floor insulation and interior thermal mass. To ensure that the energy from solar gain is modulated and stored and does not result in overheating, it is critical to have a large thermal mass exposed to solar heat. In many cases, a slab on grade requires little excavation work and can accommodate challenging site conditions such as ledge, which was present with this house.

The wall section is made up of a load-bearing 2×4 stud wall insulated with dense-pack cellulose and 8-in.-thick EPS SIPs wrapped around the exterior. The R-value of this assembly is about R-50, with almost no thermal bridging. In addition, it's easy to air-seal. This approach also enables all the

mechanical, electrical, and plumbing systems to be run through the 2×4 wall conventionally, as opposed to creating chases in the SIPs. Finally, the SIPs install quickly, and because they are factory-cut, there is less site waste.

We like to use raised-heel trusses for our roof construction because they are cost-effective and easy to install. We blow 24 in. of cellulose onto our attic floors. In addition to the insulation, we install a layer of ZIP System sheathing on the underside of the trusses and tape the seams. This layer provides an

SIX ELEMENTS OF A BETTER HOME

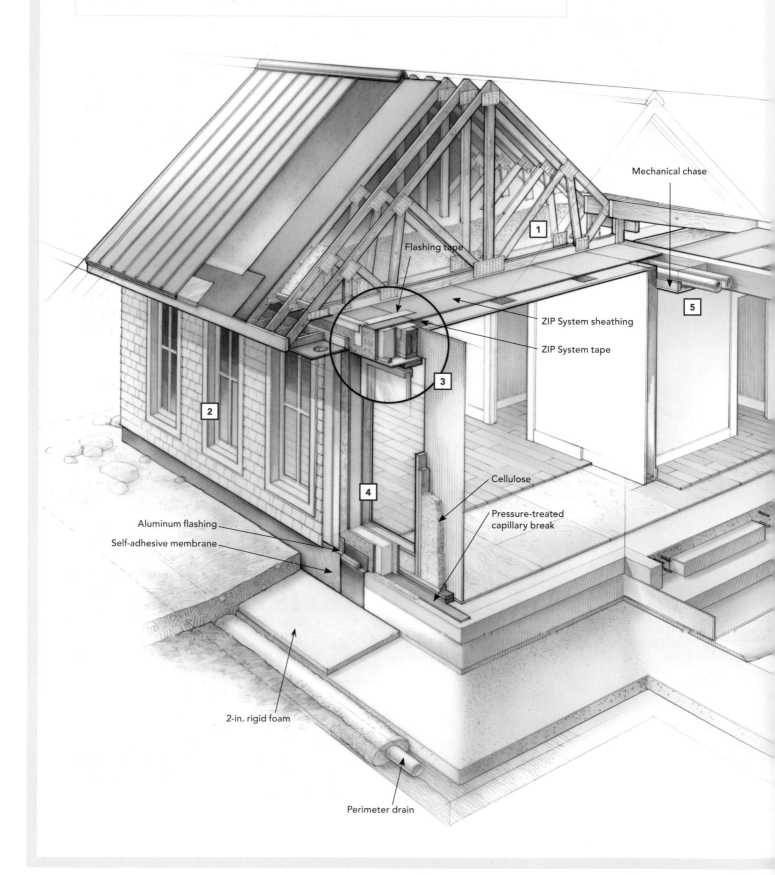

Mechanical chase

1

ZIP System sheathing

ZIP System tape

5

Flashing tape

3

2

4

Cellulose

Pressure-treated
capillary break

Aluminum flashing

Self-adhesive membrane

2-in. rigid foam

Perimeter drain

G•O Logic's approach is based on a highly insulated, airtight building shell that makes use of solar gain to lower space-heating demands, allowing the cost and complexity of the mechanical systems to be minimized. The cost savings can be invested in envelope improvements. To achieve the results O'Malia and his team are after, they need to address six critical building details.

1 INSULATION

To help keep interior temperatures at a constant and comfortable 70°F, 24 in. of cellulose (R-84) fills the attic floor, 8-in.-thick EPS-filled SIPs and a 2×4 bearing wall insulated with dense-pack cellulose create an R-50 wall assembly, and 12 in. of EPS rigid insulation below the slab yields an R-60 foundation.

2 WINDOWS

Windows typically account for one-third to one-half of a home's heat loss. For that reason alone, O'Malia uses triple-glazed windows with thermally broken frames to reduce heat loss.

3 AIR-SEALING

ZIP System wall sheathing is attached beneath the roof trusses, and its seams are taped to reduce air movement through the ceiling. Flashing tape seals the top of the wall assembly and the seams between the SIPs. Self-adhesive membrane is used to seal the subslab poly vapor barrier to the SIPs.

4 THERMAL BRIDGING

The principal components used to reduce thermal bridging through the walls are the SIPs. By reducing heat transfer through the walls and minimizing cold spots that can lead to condensation, SIPs provide a more complete thermal boundary than stick-framed walls. In addition, the stick-framing in the shed roof and the roof trusses in the main gable are spaced 24 in. on center to reduce the amount of lumber in the roof and wall assemblies, which further reduces thermal bridging.

5 VENTILATION

A heat-recovery ventilator (HRV) draws outside air into a heat-exchanging core, where it is warmed by conditioned interior-exhaust air. In this house, air is pulled through the HRV from the kitchen and bathrooms and fresh air is supplied to the main living room and the bedroom closet. The ductwork is housed in a chase beneath the insulated attic floor.

6 THERMAL MASS

A concrete slab is the most cost-effective way of storing solar energy and slowly releasing it into the living space over time. The 5-in.-thick slab is insulated to R-60 at its nonthickened portions with 12 in. of EPS foam. Superinsulating the slab prevents solar energy from leaking into the ground or through its 11-in.-thick perimeter. A 2-in.-thick layer of rigid foam surrounding the slab keeps the ground sufficiently warm and keeps the slab from heaving and cracking.

LESSON LEARNED

In this house we added 6 in. of rigid insulation instead of compacted gravel under the nonthickened portions of the slab to increase the insulation levels to R-60. It was quick and easy to install, but it made installing the subslab plumbing difficult. We'll go back to adding gravel directly beneath the slab, despite the R-value reduction.

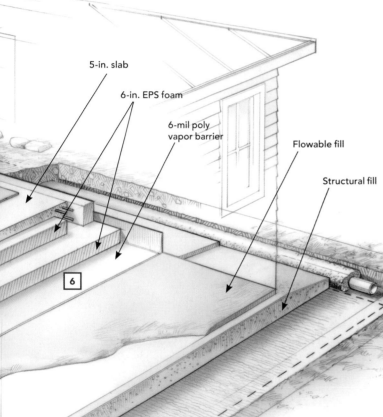

5-in. slab

6-in. EPS foam

6-mil poly vapor barrier

Flowable fill

Structural fill

6

BASIC BUT BEAUTIFUL. This bath, one of two, features a deep soaking tub beneath multiple windows. Full of function, the space also creates a getaway within the compact floor plan. Photo taken at D on floor plan.

air barrier above the conditioned living space. The air barrier also controls moisture transfer through the roof assembly, but we install soffit and gable-end vents anyway to reduce the potential of condensation on the underside of the roof deck.

The beauty of this type of design and construction is that if the building shell is built well and oriented correctly, then the house needs little heating or cooling to be comfortable year-round. The super-insulation and the thermal mass maintain a constant interior temperature. As a result, the main mechanical system for the house is not the heating system but the ventilation system, which ensures tempered fresh air throughout the house. For about $200 a year, a few sections of electric-resistance baseboard

make sure that the house stays at 70°F. When planning a ventilation system, we place the supply of fresh air in the bedrooms and living spaces and exhaust stale air from where moisture and smells are created most—in the bathrooms and kitchen.

Don't sacrifice aesthetics

Even when working within the constraints of a tight budget, we acknowledge the value of creating inviting, attractive spaces. We allocate larger portions of the budget to finishes and materials that will experience the most use, such as flooring, countertops, and bathroom fixtures and materials. Accommodating wear and tear and moisture successfully means that over time the surfaces within the home develop a desirable patina.

Downsizing brought the homeowners' actual needs into clear focus, which is also reflected in the home's design. For instance, they recognized that cooking would never be an elaborate affair in their new home. We also followed the clients' lead in developing the materials palette for the house. The intent was to keep the interior clean and simple so that the focus on the surrounding landscape would be maintained, but also to introduce a few beautiful, natural accents, such as the white-oak floor and kitchen cabinets and the soapstone countertops. The bathrooms are modestly adorned with simple white wainscot, pedestal sinks, and floor tiles to evoke a traditional cottage style common along the Maine coast.

That idea is reflected on the exterior as well. We used cedar shingles for the walls that will weather to a silver gray and that denote coastal living. To conserve money, we opted not to install any elaborate trim details. However, we did flare a wall section on the front of the house to create an eave above the large windows. This detail protects the windows from rain, but it also hints at the high level of craftsmanship put into this house. Less-expensive exterior finishes could have been selected, but this is not a cheap home. It's an inexpensive home, designed to be attractive and uncomplicated to build.

OUR CHOICE FOR HIGH-PERFORMANCE WINDOWS

GIVEN MAINE'S CLIMATE, we use triple-pane windows with glazing that accepts at least 50 percent of the sun's energy. Several windows from North American and European manufacturers meet these requirements. However, we have found that for their performance, quality, finishes, and operability, EGE windows from Germany (EGE.de/en) are our most cost-competitive option. We import them directly.

PASSIVE IMPACT. Large tilt-turn windows that meet strict Passive House standards open the living room to summer breezes, but they also have the ability to keep cold Maine winters at bay. Photo taken at E on floor plan

The Neighbor
Out Back

BY MICHAEL FIFIELD

anna Yoshimura is a Japanese artist who spends most of the year near Tokyo. When summer comes along, she returns to Eugene, Oregon, where she owns a house that she rents out. Her tenants aren't displaced when she returns, though. Hanna moves into this studio in the back-yard to live and work while she's here.

At a compact 269 sq. ft. (including lofts), the stu-dio apartment demanded a commodious design. An 11-ft. by 12-ft. workspace at the heart of the studio is bordered on each side by support spaces: a bathroom and a utility closet to the east, and a kitchen and a clothes closet to the west. The south wall is about half glass, with a pair of French doors that open onto a small deck. This garden connection, along with views of neighboring gardens from the kitchen and bath, extends sightlines and gives the studio a roomy feel.

In the summer, operable clerestory windows make it easy to take advantage of cooling breezes as they cross ventilate the studio in the evening. The exposed concrete floor provides a high-mass surface that takes on cool-breeze temperatures overnight, helping to moderate rising daytime temperatures.

THE SHOWER IS THE ROOM. A handheld shower wand, waterproof finishes, and a floor drain turn the bathroom into a shower when the doors slide shut. Photo taken at B on floor plan.

A LITTLE HOME AWAY FROM HOME. (facing page) Tucked in a corner of the backyard, this 269-sq.-ft. studio apartment includes bed, bath, kitchen, and workspace. A glass canopy over the deck protects the entry and lets in light no matter what the weather. Photo taken at C on floor plan.

154

SLEEPING LOFT ABOVE, KITCHEN BELOW. The concrete floor is incised with control joints to resemble a "good luck" tatami-mat pattern. Operable windows over the workbench and the south-facing doors foster cross ventilation. Photo taken at A on floor plan.

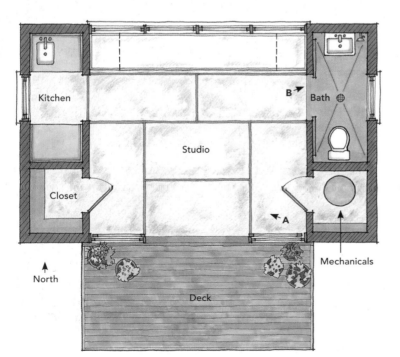

WORKSPACE/SUPPORT SPACE

The center of the studio is dedicated to art projects, and the workspace can expand outward to include the front deck when the weather is good. Sleeping lofts over the kitchen and bath complete the plan.

Photos taken at lettered positions.

A Tiny Traditional Japanese House

BY CHARLES BICKFORD

I n a small town north of Seattle, three carpenters devoted six months to building a house in the traditional Japanese style for a local aikido teacher. Although it was a group project, the job took shape under the careful eye of Dale Brotherton, who apprenticed with a teahouse builder in California for seven years and later practiced traditional joinery in Japan for two years.

The woods used in the project were all local species and hand-planed, rather than sanded, to a smooth perfection. The builders used Ponderosa pine for floorboards, Port Orford cedar for posts and interior trim, Douglas fir for framing, and western red cedar for the exterior. The interior walls were finished with a type of plaster known as *juraku*, a troweled-on stucco finish that emulates the traditional *tsuchi-kabe* (earth wall), a clay/straw/sand mix. Above the board-and-batten siding, the exterior walls were coated with a form of acrylic stucco.

ELEMENTS OF A COUNTRY HOUSE. Although smaller than most houses, the house still possesses many design features found in traditional Japanese architecture, including deep exposed roof overhangs, and sliding window panels.

JOINERY SERVES DOUBLE DUTY AS ORNAMENTATION. (below) Haunched-tusk tenons intersect and support one corner of the second-floor tie beams. As in much of the house, the joints here are held in place by wedges and pins, not glue.

ONE ROOM OF SIMPLE CONTRASTS. (above) The house's exposed interior framing demonstrates the contrast between unmilled cedar logs and the precise joinery and smooth finishes of milled lumber. The understair storage (*kaidan dansu*) is made of cherry and white pine; the charcoal brazier (*irori*), framed with cherry and fir, is only decorative here.

BEDROOM STORAGE DOESN'T CLUTTER THE FLOOR. (above) Hidden behind sliding screens, clothing and personal items are kept in wall closets rather than in trunks or bureaus, keeping the floor plan relatively simple.

GREETING VISITORS. An orna-mental garden and gate signal the homes traditional Japanese heritage.

PART 4

Sheds, Studios,
and Other Small Structures

The Watershed:
A Writing Studio

BY ERIN MOORE

My family owns a small piece of former pastureland in central Oregon. When my parents asked me to design a writing studio for the property, I worried that putting a building there would tarnish its ecological richness—that we would commit the age-old blunder of ruining a rare place by wanting to live right on it.

We talked over the question of building something for a couple of years. My family is a tough jury. My brother and my father are a research ecologist and a biologist, respectively, and my mother is an environmental philosopher and a nature writer. We all had a stake in the integrity of our tiny nature preserve, my mother needed a place to do her work, and I wanted to test out some new design ideas.

Our discussions unearthed two questions that became my design challenges: What kind of writing studio could we build without bringing a road or electricity to the site? And what could we build that would also disappear conveniently at the end of its useful life?

Before I finished the design, we took turns sitting in a chair on the hillside where the studio would be. We chose our favorite views, narrowed those down to just a handful, and then carefully measured where the openings should be to define them best.

The large window over the desk is the most traditional. It frames a moderately distant view of the field and the riparian forest. The high window at the rear frames a bit of sky in which there is often a raptor taking advantage of a local updraft.

Opposite the door is a very low window about 18 in. square that is meant to draw your eye to a patch of grass just outside—a view that is not extraordinary until you look closely and discover something like a new bloom or a cricket. It is easy to track seasonal changes in the color of the grasses through this window. It's also my 2-year-old niece's favorite.

SITTING LIGHTLY ON, AND IN, THE LANDSCAPE.
Nested inside a prefabricated steel framework, this
diminutive writing studio overlooks a meadow. The
studio's butterfly roof directs runoff into a trough that
serves as the local watering hole (facing page).

THE CEDAR POSTS ARE BOLTED TO FLANGES WELDED TO THE STEEL FRAME.
Tongue-and-groove siding slips into grooves plowed in the sides of the cedar posts,
making walls that can expand, contract, and breathe well in this damp climate.

ROOM WITH A VIEW.
The big window above
the writing desk frames
a riparian forest in the
distance, while below
the desk, awning-style
hinged panels rise
to welcome meadow
breezes.

A CEDAR BOX INSIDE A STEEL EXOSKELETON

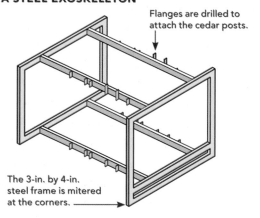

Flanges are drilled to
attach the cedar posts.

The 3-in. by 4-in.
steel frame is mitered
at the corners.

Prefabricated for easy assembly on site

A quartet of concrete piers supports the studio. We
cast the piers in place, with many hands making
light work of it. We didn't miss having an electric-
powered concrete mixer; instead, we put the
concrete on a tarp and mixed it by pulling up on
the corners.

The second stage—the structure—is a single
freestanding steel armature. We had it fabricated in
a metal shop, and then moved it to our woodshop
where we cut and dry-fit the cedar skin and the polycarbonate roof to the frame. Then we took it back to
its bare bones and moved the frame to the site with a
front-loader. It can be removed the same way when it
is no longer needed.

We brought the rest of the parts to the site by
foot, where we made final adjustments with battery-
powered tools. The trail we blazed as we carried each
piece is now the footpath to the studio, which we call
the "watershed" for its rain-gathering roof and for
the larger watershed that it inhabits, at least for now.

Baking Studio Alfresco

BY RUTH LIVELY

When cookbook author Fran Gage was making plans for her new wood-fired oven, she envisioned it out in the open, surrounded by a circle of redwood trees, just steps from the Gages' weekend house on a mountainside above Navarro, California. But when friend and architect Bob Hersey suggested the oven would be more useful if sheltered from the area's winter rains, Fran agreed. So he designed a 15-ft.-square building with three walls of glass and wide sliding doors. While they were at it, the Gages decided they might as well have a sink, a couple of gas burners, and room for a table and chairs, in addition to Fran's worktable. And thus a bread baking studio was born.

Inside and out, the completed baking studio is a study in functional simplicity. The spare style and large expanses of glass offer the best of both worlds—protection from the elements and a direct link to the beauty of the outdoors. "The building is almost transparent," says Hersey, "and from inside you're very aware of the surrounding redwoods."

The framing and exterior siding are redwood; interior woodwork is Douglas fir. The floor and counter are concrete treated with a clear sealant. Fran and her husband Sidney concocted the hanging lamps with parts from the hardware store. The

NESTLED IN A CIRCLE OF REDWOOD TREES, Fran Gage's 225-sq.-ft. baking studio houses a wood-fired oven, a sink, a two-burner stove, a worktable, a counter, and storage space, plus a dining area. A louvered cupola draws excess heat from the room. The studio is a great dining and entertaining space, guaranteed to be cozy even in chilly weather.

wood-fired brick-and-plaster oven, made by Petaluma oven builder Alan Scott, dominates one corner of the room. The Gages have discovered that the studio is great for entertaining. Fran says, "Baking with wood is a slow and ancient process that allows us to enjoy long evenings with friends."

BAKING IN THE REDWOODS.
Although no longer a professional baker, Fran Gage fans
the flames of her passion in a
small building at the family's
weekend retreat. It takes
about four hours to heat the
oven, but one firing is enough
to bake bread, roast some
ducks and a vegetable gratin,
bake a fruit tart, and finally
slow-cook lamb shanks and
beans overnight.

A Tree House That's for the Birds

BY MAUREEN FRIEDMAN

Needing a spare room for occasional overnight guests, ornithologist Alan Poole first thought about building a yurt on his wooded lot. Poole asked contractor and fellow bird-watcher Mike Sylvia of Right Angel Restoration to tackle the project. Rather than a yurt, Sylvia suggested that Poole consider building a tree house that could be used for nature watching as well as housing guests. Poole, the author of *Ospreys: A Natural and Unnatural History* and the editor of *The Birds of North America*, says that Sylvia didn't have to work hard to get him to agree.

Set approximately 12 ft. above ground, the tree house is constructed of rough pine supplied by a local sawmill, recycled windows and doors, and a metal roof. The platform measures 16 ft. by 16 ft. and the house is 10 ft. by 12 ft. Sylvia used Garnier Limb® brackets (www.treehouses.com) to affix the supports for the tree house to the trees. These brackets allow the tree to continue growing and enable the structure to sway gently in the wind. Sylvia built the tree house in addition to doing most of the design work. At Poole's suggestion, Sylvia added bunk beds constructed from cedar for overnight guests and a porch for sitting and practicing yoga.

STEPPING LIGHTLY.
Built with brackets that enable the trees to continue growing and with a railing contoured around nearby tree trunks, this small house treads lightly on the land while taking full advantage of its surroundings.

Teatime in Wisconsin

BY MAUREEN FRIEDMAN

Homeowners Jim and Cheryl Smeja wanted to build a teahouse in their backyard that appeared to float on water like a lily pad. A collaborative effort involving designer Amber Westerman, carpenter Randolph Fleming, and landscaper Larry Terrill was able to make this happen. The slope of the yard made the illusion possible, with construction of an upper pond with waterfalls dropping to a pool below.

The teahouse rests on a reinforced-concrete foundation with wings covered with a limestone veneer extending on each side to hold back the upper pond. Pressure-treated floor joists laid on the sill plate cantilever 3 ft. beyond the foundation to create a walkway around the house. The decking is plantation-grown ipé. Above, a double layer of rafters creates a two-tiered roof, which is sheathed with 2×8 Douglas fir boards alternating with bamboo and covered with cedar shingles. The projecting rafter tails extend just beyond the decking; the 6½-ft. clearance creates a heightened sense of shelter and keeps out rain. Lag screws and nails are concealed behind wood plugs.

Each wall of the teahouse is composed of four custom-made screened doors created by Joel Duncanson and set between corner posts. The two middle doors hang on a concealed metal track at the top and slip into wood runners attached to the deck at the bottom, allowing a 6-ft. center opening on each side. The lower exterior panel of each door is wood detailed to look like stucco; the interior is covered with grass cloth.

IT'S IN THE DETAILS. Built over a constructed koi pond with custom-made rolling screen doors created by Joel Duncanson, the teahouse offers an enchanting getaway.

Off the Grid, on the Shore

BY MAUREEN FRIEDMAN

Five years after architect Obie Bowman designed their home on the Oregon coast, former clients approached him to design a year-round, multipurpose building to complement the house. They wanted a greenhouse and writing studio that would suit the rugged surroundings, stand up to

coastal storms, and allow them to enjoy the ocean views. The structure had to be low maintenance and self-sufficient, and be built from sustainable, environmentally friendly materials. A tall order for a small building, perhaps, but Bowman rose to the challenge and conceived the Garden House.

The 325-sq.-ft. structure's concrete-mat foundation and log-beam buttresses can easily withstand the 90-mph winds howling off the ocean. Bowman used locally harvested Port Orford cedar, salvaged and recycled horizontal slat siding, and corrugated sheet metal for the building's exterior and roofing. In one of the most interesting touches, he backed the inside of the sheathing with sheet metal and used the 2×10 studs and blocking to create niches and shelving for storage and display.

The off-the-grid building is powered by a combination of integrated and remote photovoltaic panels. Battery storage provides AC power for lighting, outlets, and pumps that bring water to the outbuilding from a nearby shallow well. Condensation and rainwater from the roof also help to keep the two holding tanks full.

SUSTAINABLE DESIGN. The large windows provide abundant natural light and in combination with the dark concrete floors, the space is kept warm.

An Old-Time Garden Shed

BY DAVID EDRINGTON

There's no obvious connection between burying utility lines and putting up a garden shed, but that's what happened at our house. After years of trying to get the power company to streamline a patchwork of wires that crossed over our backyard, the work finally happened. It meant that at last we could improve our yard without worrying about a trench carving it up in the future.

So we fixed the drainage; terraced the slopes; and built rock walls, a brick patio, and a pergola. We also left a spot in the southeast corner for a garden shed.

Make It More Than a Storage Bin

Initially the shed's purpose was to store garden tools and supplies that were clogging the garage. Its role evolved into a place where we also could have tea and maybe even camp out with the grandchildren. The shed's most important purpose, however, was to anchor the corner of the yard visually, giving shape to a series of roomlike outdoor spaces.

Starting points for the design included a porch (teatime shelter on a rainy Oregon morning), a steep roof (18-in-12 pitch to relate the shed to the steep roof of the existing house), and no modern construction materials. We did use a modern design tool, though. Creating the design in SketchUp® let us build the shed on-screen, right down to the number of studs. Our builder, Marv Glover, used both two- and three-dimensional views as he assembled the shed.

A TINY BUILDING WITH A BIG PRESENCE. In the southeast corner of the lot, at its highest point, the garden shed helps to define the borders of distinct outdoor spaces, including a formal garden with a fountain at its center.

MAKE IT LOOK OLD.
Exposed framing with diagonal sheathing harkens back to early-20th-century building practices. Recycled windows, an old Dutch door, and used brick emphasize the rustic feel.

ALMOST LIKE A FOUR-POSTER BED. (below) Surrounded by bracketed posts, the porch extends the architectural details and colors that characterize the main house into the backyard.

IT'S A SLEEPOVER SHED. (above) Camp-style beds in the loft slip into dormers on both sides of the steep roof. The hatch in the floor between them leads to a pull-down ladder for access.

Construction notes

The shed's rectangular footprint measures 8 ft. 6 in. by 12 ft. 6 in.; a 4-ft.-6-in.-deep porch faces the yard. Stick-framed with 2×4s, the shed is sheathed with 1×10 pine boards applied diagonally and exposed on the inside as finished walls. All 12 windows are made from recycled sash. An extrawide pull-down stair leads to a loft, which has dormers front and back. We built a bed into each dormer, with storage underneath.

We compromised a bit on our old-materials-only directive. Besides an electrical system, we installed 1½-in. foil-faced rigid insulation under the roof and wall shingles to boost thermal performance. We also mixed our own weathered green stain for the shingles and used gloss enamel paint on the trim and other exposed wood.

The shed is a pleasure to look at any time we're in the garden, and it's a wonderful retreat from the house. We love it. The grandchildren love it. In the summer, it is the last spot in the garden to be hit by the late-evening sunset. It glows.

Studio, Storage, and More

BY MAUREEN FRIEDMAN

Don't let the pretty face and cozy interior of this little structure fool you; it's actually Deborah and Norman Lee's backyard storage building. This hardworking shed, christened "the cottage" by the Lees, is a marvel at multitasking. The 9½-ft. by 6-ft. interior provides plenty of wintertime storage for deck and patio furniture. When warm weather arrives, interior decorator Deb moves her drafting table and a comfy daybed into the space and the storage area is transformed into the perfect outdoor studio. The shed's windows and door were salvaged from a neighbor's renovation project, and the shed's roof is outfitted with a rainwater-collection system for the Lees' gardens. As an added bonus, the Lees agree there's no better place for watching the sunset at "happy hour" than the inviting bistro set on the cottage's deck.

BEYOND STORAGE. The shed's inviting deck is surrounded by the homeowners' garden and is the perfect spot to enjoy the sunset.

Shinto Shed

BY MAUREEN FRIEDMAN

UNIQUE HARDWARE.
Montgomery designed
and fabricated the custom
door pulls and hinges.

The extreme simplicity of the ancient *shinmei-zukuri* style of Japanese architecture inspired Glenn Montgomery's 9-ft. by 12-ft. shed. This shed is based on the design of Japan's Ise Grand Shrine. Montgomery built much of the shed from reclaimed materials. These included 6×16 old-growth timbers salvaged during a renovation of Denver's original Neusteter's department store, and semi-rotten 2×6 decking that Montgomery culled, denailed, ripped, and rabbeted to create the red-wood siding. The steel platform was salvaged from commercial-foundation lagging, and the joists are repurposed Unistrut® rescued from job-site roll-off containers. New corrugated galvanized roofing, glazing, fasteners, and some steel plate rounded out Montgomery's materials list.

Early in the shed's design phase, Montgomery decided that the large overhang would make a good shelter for new finds that were destined for his shed and, once that was completed, future projects. With each load of salvaged materials, Montgomery reassures his patient wife, Debbie, that he will "build something with it someday." But as everyone knows, job-site salvage can't just be taken home and reused immediately. It must be seasoned for at least five years.

The Benefits of a Smaller Scale

BY MAUREEN FRIEDMAN
AND CHARLES BICKFORD

The beauty of a tiny building is that it can be a quick way to try out a new design, color scheme, or building technique. Even if you get extravagant, it's hard to break the bank in 35 sq. ft. And in the end, you get a place to store your lawn mower or to nurture your inner hermit. Here are some examples, both great and small, from backyards around the country.

NO WRITER'S BLOCK HERE. Incorporating driftwood framing, recycled materials, and stained glass by Gabriella Camilleri, South Mountain Company of Martha's Vineyard made this writer's studio for an affordable-building fundraiser.

STORYBOOK SHED. (above) During cocktail hour one night, Karen Metzger sketched her ideal garden outbuilding. That was all that her husband, Greg, needed to begin work on their 8-ft. by 12-ft. shed. Built mostly with salvaged materials, the shed has top-hinged windows for ventilation, a gable and loft for storage, an oversize rear door for bringing in large equipment, a potting bench, and even a place to display the antlers they found in the woods.

DRESSING UP THE BOILER ROOM. On Orcas Island, Washington, designer/builder Chris Morris made a one-man show of this outbuilding that houses a nearby hot tub's changing room and wood-fired boiler.

GOTHIC DAIRY-BARN SHED. (left)"Labor intensive but fun to build" is how Philip Bowman describes his barn-style shed. Bowman kept the shed to 120 sq. ft. to meet his city's building code for a nonpermitted shed, but its large loft area provides plenty of space for lumber storage. To achieve the desired roof shape, he wet ½-in. plywood to bend it. He admits that a lot of bandsaw and router work was required to accomplish his task.

DON'T BURN IT, BUILD WITH IT. (right) Located on an island off the coast of British Columbia, this small building designed and built by Netonia Yalte is an example of cordwood masonry, walls built with short lengths of logs with concrete infill.

THE QUEEN'S MAGICAL SHED. Using the remains of projects "full of goodness," Rory McDonnell constructed this shed full of "good light and air circulation." Too lovely to be used for storing the lawn mower and out-of-season sporting goods, the shed was claimed by McDonnell's wife, Catherine, as a tree-sheltered retreat for dreaming, napping, and creating art.

CEDAR-SHAKE GARDEN SHED. Built on piers so that it could be moved with a forklift if needed, this garden shed was built for the owner's new riding mower. The walls were sided with cedar shakes to match the house and were painted dark green to minimize the visual impact in a tree-filled yard. False windows were installed to add interest to the otherwise plain walls. Homeowner Nick Poepping says the shed was a "fun project and definitely adds a focal point" to his wife's flower gardens.

LET'S PLAY HOUSE. Thanks to an unknown carpenter, there are some children who will grow up with a well-grounded sense of Victorian shingle-work.

POTTING SHED AND MORE. What began as a simple shed evolved into a 16-ft. by 20-ft. outbuilding. A 12-ft. by 24-ft. shed-roof extension wraps around the rear and side to shelter tractors and yard tools, the east-wall window provides natural light for a potting station, and a loft has storage for an "endless pile of construction debris" from ongoing projects. The doors, windows, and finish materials reflect design elements in the house and barn.

SHED FOR A MODERN GLASS HOUSE. Architect Mark LePage says this shed (far right of the main house) "turned out to be one of our favorite projects." After his company completed a full restoration of a 1969 contemporary house, the homeowners requested that his company design and build a modern shed to complement the house and pool.

IT'S ALL ABOUT THE GRASS. Running on a theme of less wood, Dan Neelands built this utility building with straw-bale walls and a sod roof.

CONTRIBUTORS

Charles Bickford is a *Fine Home-building* senior editor.

Anne Corey is a former *Inspired House* assistant editor.

David Edrington is an architect and frequent contributor to *Fine Homebuilding*. He's based in Eugene, Ore.

Chris Ermides is a former *Fine Homebuilding* associate editor. In addition to writing and carpentry he fills his time as a freelance web producer for Taunton's Workshop e-learnng series. He lives in Saratoga Springs, NY with his wife and two sons.

David Evans has a design practice in Boulder, Colo.

Michael Fifield, FAIA, is a principal in Fifield Architecture + Urban Design, and a Professor/ Co-Director of the Housing Focus in the Department of Architecture at the University of Oregon in Eugene.

Maureen Friedman is the *Fine Homebuilding* administrative assistant.

Timothy Gordon lives in Portland, Ore., where he practices architecture. Whenever possible, he spends time on the Oregon coast, in the house he designed for his mother.

Tina Govan, (www.tinagovan .com) is principal of Tina Govan Architect, Inc. in Raleigh, NC.

Russell Hamlet is a principal at Studio Hamlet Architects (www .studiohamlet.com), an innovative and environmentally focused architecture firm based on Bainbridge Island, Wash.

Matt Hutchins is a principal at CAST architecture in Seattle (www.CASTarchitecture.com).

Robert Knight is an architect in Blue Hill, Maine.

Maria LaPiana is a former *Inspired House* associate editor.

Ruth Lively is a former *Fine Gardening* and *Kitchen Gardener* editor and is the author of *Taunton's Complete Guide to Growing Vegetables and Herbs* (Taunton Press, 2011).

Charles Miller worked as an editor for *Fine Homebuilding* for more than 30 years. After his retirement, he moved to California, but he remains on the masthead as an editor at large.

Erin Moore is an assistant professor of architecture at the University of Oregon and principal of FLOAT (www.floatwork.com).

Matthew O'Malia is a partner at G•O Logic in Belfast, Maine.

Justin Pauly is an architect with a practice based in Monterey, Calif. He studied architecture at U.C. Berkeley.

Nir Pearlson practices architecture in Eugene Ore, specializing in low-impact and small-home design.

Parker Platt is a principal at Platt Architecture (www .plattarchitecture.com) in Brevard, N.C.

Samara Rafert is a former *Inspired House* editorial assistant.

Debra Judge Silber is the *Fine Homebuilding* managing editor.

Sigrid Simonson a former sportswear designer, is now the Vice President and Creative Director for Brentwood Originals, a manufacturer of decorative indoor and outdoor pillows for the major mass market retailers.

Sarah Susanka a best-selling author, architect, and cultural visionary, is leading a movement that is redefining the American home. Her "build better, not bigger" approach to residential design has been embraced by millions. She is a member of the College of Fellows of the American Institute of Architects and a Senior Fellow of the Design Futures Council. More about her work and her Not So Big® House series of books at www. notsobighouse.com.

Jesse Thompson is an architect in Portland, Maine. He is a LEED Accredited Professional and a Certified Passive House Consultant at Kaplan Thompson Architects (www.kaplanthompson.com).

Roxana Vargas-Greenan and Trent Greenan live in Oakland, Calif. Their firm is Vargas Greenan Architecture - Civic Design (www.vargasgreenan.com).

Peter Kurt Woerner, FAIA, is an architect and builder based in New Haven, Conn.

Jonathan White is a builder and writer based on Orcas Island, Wash.

CREDITS

All photos are courtesy of *Fine Home-building* magazine (FHB) © The Taunton Press, Inc., or *Inspired House* magazine (IH), © The Taunton Press, Inc., except as noted below:

pp. 2–7: Not So Big Solutions: How much space do you really need? by Sarah Susanka, IH issue 14 and In your new house, how much space do you really need? by Sarah Susanka, IH issue 15. Illustrations by Sarah Susanka, colored by Christine Erikson

pp. 10–15: A Big Little House on the Ridge by Jonathan White, FHB issue 171. Photos by Charles Miller. Drawings by Paul Perreault.

pp. 16–20: Raising the Baby Barn by Peter Kurt Woerner, FHB issue 179. Photos and drawings by Peter Kurt Woerner except for photos pp. 19 and 20 by Bill Seitz.

pp. 21–27: Did Starting Small Work Out? by Robert Knight, FHB issue 219. Photos by Charles Miller except for photos pp. 21, 22 (top), and 23 (right) by Robert Knight. Floor-plan and elevation drawings by Martha Garstang Hill. Drawings p. 26 courtesy of Robert Knight.

pp. 28–30: Getaways: Watch Island retreat by Inspired House staff, IH issue 1. Photos by Randy O'Rourke. Drawing by Martha Garstang Hill.

pp. 31–33: Getaways: Nestled in the trees by Inspired House staff, IH issue 3. Photos by davidduncanlivingston.com. Drawing by Martha Garstang Hill.

pp. 34–36: Getaways: A place to read and relax by Anne Corey, IH issue 4. Photos by Norman McGrath. Drawing by Martha Garstang Hill.

pp. 37–39: Getaways: Legacy on the lake by Maria LaPiana, IH issue 6. Photos by davidduncanlivingston.com.

pp. 40–42: Getaways: Do-it-yourself retreat by Samara Rafert, IH issue 8. Photos by Mike Jensen. Drawings by Martha Garstang Hill.

p. 43: Cranking Up the View by Chris Ermides, FHB issue 184. Photos by Benjamin Benschneider.

pp. 44–45: At Home in the Woods by Chris Ermides, FHB issue 192. Photos by Benjamin Benschneider.

pp. 46–47: Finishing Touch: The Crib by Maureen Friedman, FHB issue 237. Photos by Anice Hoachlander.

p. 48: Chainsaw Tour de Forest by Chris Ermides, FHB issue 180. Photos by Paul Joseph.

pp. 50–57: A Garden Cottage for Low-Impact Living by Nir Pearlson, FHB issue 235. Photos by mikedeanphoto .com. Drawings by Martha Garstang Hill.

pp. 58–62: The Second Time Around by Charles Bickford, FHB issue 220. Photos by Brian Vanden Brink except for photo p. 59 courtesy of South Mountain Co. Drawings by Martha Garstang Hill.

pp. 63-69: Small Cottage Makes a Big Splash by David Evans, FHB issue 162. Photos by Roe A. Osborn except for photo p. 66 (bottom) courtesy of Invisible Structures. Drawings by Paul Perreault.

pp. 70–77: A Higher Standard by Jesse Thompson, FHB issue 235. Photos by Trent Bell. Floor-plan drawings by Martha Garstang Hill; construction drawing by John Hartman.

pp. 78–83: Carriage-House Comeback by Matt Hutchins, FHB issue 227. Photos by Charles Miller except for photo p. 83 (bottom right) by Rob Yagid. Drawings by Martha Garstang Hill.

pp. 84–91: Spall & Spacious by Timothy Gordon, IH issue 8. Photos by Philip Clayton-Thompson. Drawings by Martha Garstang Hill.

pp. 92–93: Design Gallery: Timeless Character by Sarah Susanka, FHB issue 227. Photos by Brian Vanden Brink.

pp. 94–97: A Cottage Fit for a Hobbit by Debra Judge Silber, FHB issue 186. Photos courtesy of Archer & Buchanan.

pp. 99–105: Small-House Secrets by Charles Miller, FHB issue 238. Photos by Charles Miller except for photos p. 105 by David Wakely. Drawing by Martha Garstang Hill.

pp. 106–111: Big River, Small House by Russell Hamlet, FHB issue 211. Photos by Charles Miller except for photo p. 110 (left) courtesy of Russell Hamlet. Drawings by Martha Garstang Hill.

pp. 112–119: Passive House Perfection by Justin Pauly, FHB issue 235. Photos by Rob Yagid except for photo p. 113 by Rich Pharaoh. House plan drawings by Martha Garstang Hill; construction drawings by Don Mannes.

pp. 120–124: A Small, Spacious House for a Skinny City Lot by Roxana Vargas-Greenan and Trent Greenan, FHB issue 196. Photos by John Ross. Drawings by Don Mannes.

pp. 125–-129: A Tiny Addition for a Growing Family by Tina Govan, FHB issue 197. Photos by Rob Yagid except for photos pp. 125, 126, and 129 (bottom) by James West. Drawing p. 127 (top) by Bruce Morser; drawing p. 127 (bottom) by Martha Garstang Hill.

pp. 130-137: A New Floor Plan Saves an Old House by Parker Platt, FHB issue 229. Photos by Rob Yagid except for photo p. 130 by Kevin Meechean and photos pp. 131 and 137 (top) courtesy of Parker Platt. Drawings by Dan Thornton.

pp. 138–145: A Better House Not a Bigger One by Sigrid Simonson, IH issue 14. Photos by Jennifer Cheung. Drawings by Martha Garstang Hill.

pp. 146–153: Build Like This by Matthew O'Malia, FHB issue 232. Photos by Brian Vanden Brink. Floor plan drawing by Martha Garstang Hill; construction drawing by Bruce Morser.

pp. 154–156: Design Gallery: The neighbor out back by Michael Fifield, FHB issue 203. Photos by mikedeanphoto.com. Drawing by Martha Garstang Hill.

pp. 157–158: Finishing Touches: Too big for a jewel box, almost too small for a house, by Charles Bickford, FHB issue 136. Photos by Charles Bickford.

pp. 160–162: Design Gallery: The watershed by Erin Moore, FHB issue 203. Photos by J. Gary Tarleton except for photo p. 162 (top) by Frank Moore. Drawing by Erin Moore.

pp. 163–165: Getaways: Baking studio alfresco by Ruth Lively, IH issue 2. Photos by Saxon Holt.

pp. 166–167: Finishing Touch: A tree house that's fit for the birds by Maureen Friedman, FHB issue 236. Photos by Nat Rea.

pp. 168–169: Project Gallery: Great work outdoors by Maureen Friedman, FHB issue 229. Photos courtesy of Cheryl Smeja.

pp. 170–171: Off the Grid, on the Shore by Maureen Friedman, FHB issue 204. Photos by Obie Bowman.

pp. 172–174: Design Gallery: Small spaces that are great places by David Edrington, FHB issue 203. Photos by Kent Peterson. Drawing by David Edrington.

p. 175: Project Gallery: Studio, storage, and more by Maureen Friedman, issue 214. Photos by Norman Lee.

p. 176: Shinto Shed by Maureen Friedman, FHB issue 224. Photos courtesy of Charles Walters Photo.

pp. 177–181: Project Gallery: Stylish sheds by Maureen Friedman, FHB issue 224 and Finishing Touches: The benefits of a smaller scale by Charles Bickford, FHB issue 161. Photos pp. 177 and 180 (top right) by Brian Vanden Brink, photo p. 178 (top) by Karen and Greg Metzger, photos pp. 178 (bottom) and 181 (bottom) by Charles Miller, photo p. 179 (top) by Philip Bowman, photo p. 179 (center) by Peter Hemp, photo p. 179 (bottom) by Rory McDonnell, photo p. 180 (top left) by Nick Poepping, photo p. 180 (bottom) by Michael Shipe, and photo p. 181 (top) courtesy of Scott LePage Photography.

INDEX

A
Additions to existing houses, 125–130
Affordability
    as a balancing act, 124
    designing for high performance and, 147–149, 152

B
Barns
    bank, Baby Barn based on, 16–20
    shed, Gothic dairy-barn style, 179
Bathrooms
    functional and beautiful, 152
    ladder, reached by a, 15
    lighting, 83
    shower, that turn into a, 154
    upgrading and adding a master bath, 134–135

C
Cabins
    chainsaw joinery on, 48
    crank-up window in contemporary, 43
    do-it-yourself, 40–42
    factory-built, 46–47
    log, 34–36
    playful marshland, 34–36
    post-and-beam, 31–33
Carriage houses, 78–83
Ceilings
    exposed, 126
    plaster, 69
    radiant panels mounted in, 61
    raised, 100, 141–142
    vaulted, 11, 82, 83, 84, 85, 108, 109, 114
Cottages
    garden, 50–57
    for a Hobbit, 94–97
    pocket-sized, 84–91
    stacked and compact, 63–69
    21st century, 70–77
    with timeless character, 92–93
Cupolas, 19

D
Doors
    barn, 82
    custom-made rolling screen, 168, 169
    expanding the feel of a room with, 129
    French, 16, 18, 19, 31, 34, 36, 40
    glass, 84, 91
    for a Hobbit's cottage, 97
    pocket, 141
Driveways, turf surface for, 66

E
Energy efficiency and/or environmental concerns. *See* Sustainability

F
Finishes
    aesthetics and, 152
    exterior
    long-lasting, 54
    low-maintenance stucco, 64, 65–66
    Maine coast-appropriate, 76–77
    subtle for cabinets and ceilings, 101
Fireplaces
    as centerpieces, 18–19, 20, 36
    concrete sanded smooth, 33
    copper-clad, 36
    propane-fired stainless steel, 47
    Rumford, 12–13, 19, 20
Floor plan(s)
    the Baby Bank Barn, 18
    the Baer's remodel, 5
    Cathy Schwabe's small house, 102
    Craftsman-style bungalow, before and after remodeling a, 132
    David's stacked and compact cottage, 65
    function-packed, 11–13, 47
    the Govan's addition, 127
    the Green's houseboat, 107
    Hanna's studio apartment, 156
    Julie and Rob's garden cottage, 57
    the Kimballs' big little cabin, 11
    Leslie's pocket-size house, 91
    marshland cabin, 36
    Mica and Laureen's Passive House, 114
    Michael and Peg's do-it-yourself retreat, 42
    narrow urban infill house for a skinny lot, 121
    the Nobles' evolving house, phases of, 24–25
    Rob and Fiona's 21st century cottage, 73
    Sigrid and Bob's "beach house," 140
    space-saving features for a small, 60
    Wendy and Bill's sustainable retirement home, 148
    the Widners' carriage house, 80
    the Winston's new house, 7
Foundations
    floating, 110
    insulated slab-on-grade, 74, 148–149
    insulation for, 62
    sloped site and, 16
Furniture, 144–145

G
Gardens
    cottage in, 50–57
    greenhouse and writing studio, 170–171
    the home, as the crucial ingredient of, 89
    linking house and, 51
    outdoor rooms and, 78–79 (*see also* Outdoor spaces)
    potting shed, 180
    sheds for, 172–174, 178, 180
    windows overlooking, 80–81, 88
Guesthouse
    the Baby Barn, 16–20
    houseboat as, 106–111
    moving and converting a small house into, 137
    tree house as, 166–167
Guest room
    captain's bed that transforms into, 138, 139
    home office and, problem of combining 24
    quilting studio that converts into, 86

H
Handrails, 12, 13, 69
Home offices, 24, 25, 26, 86–87, 92
Houseboats, 106–111
    "Human scale," 53

I
Insulated-concrete forms (ICFs), 65